Advance Praise for *The Black Boom*

"I don't know what I liked more about *The Black Boom*: Jason Riley's persuasive, provocative, and counterintuitive analysis of how racial inequality decreased during Donald Trump's divisive presidency. Or the fact that the volume includes powerful critiques of Riley by Juan Williams and Wilfred Reilly. What I do know for sure is that this volume is a model for serious policy discussions in a country filled with shallow partisans more interested in talking past one another rather than fixing real problems."

—NICK GILLESPIE, editor at large, *Reason*

"Jason Riley's commitment to facts, impartial analysis of the data, and dedication to principled public policy have made him one of America's foremost thought leaders. Each of these traits is on full display in *The Black Boom*, in which he argues that minorities enjoyed real economic progress during the Trump administration. His case is nonpartisan, sharply reasoned, and deserving of serious attention. I highly recommend it and hope that it inspires productive dialogue that moves us beyond our divisiveness."

—DR. ARTHUR B. LAFFER, economist and
Presidential Medal of Freedom Recipient

"This important and explosive little book provides stimulation and provocation on every page, demolishing conventional wisdom about black progress in the process. Riley insists recent history demonstrates that black families have benefited far more from the opportunities provided by free-market economics than from government programs and the over-valued acquisition of political power. He writes with a combination of grace and force that may change some minds while opening many more."

—MICHAEL MEDVED, nationally syndicated
radio host, and the author of *God's Hand
on America*

The Black Boom

THE BLACK BOOM

><

By Jason L. Riley

TEMPLETON PRESS

Templeton Press
300 Conshohocken State Road, Suite 500
West Conshohocken, PA 19428
www.templetonpress.org

Set in Sabon LT Pro by Westchester Publishing Services

This paper meets the requirements of ANSI/NISO Z39.48-1992 (Permanence of Paper).

ISBN: 978-1-59947-589-9 (paperback)
ISBN: 978-1-59947-590-5 (ebook)

Library of Congress Control Number: 2021945336

A catalogue record for this book is available from the Library of Congress.

Printed in the United States of America.

22 23 24 25 26   10 9 8 7 6 5 4 3 2 1

To Paul Gigot, Dan Henninger, and the Wall Street Journal *editorial page staff, who managed to keep their cool and their principles during a period when so many others in the media did neither.*

Contents

———— ≥≤ ————

The Black Boom

Introduction

❧❧

B ELIEF THAT THE ECONOMIC advancement of racial and ethnic minority groups is conditioned on political clout and government programs is widely held, but the supporting evidence is thinner than many people realize. Historically, groups that have risen fastest from poverty into the American middle class—the Germans, Jews, and Japanese, among others—did so with little if any political power. The focus was not on electing "their own" to office but rather on developing the human capital—the education, skills, work habits, and attitudes—that facilitates upward mobility.

By comparison, the Irish who arrived in the mid-nineteenth century enjoyed tremendous political success while simultaneously lagging economically. By the late 1900s, Irish political machines were operating in cities from San Francisco to Chicago to Boston. Financially, however, the Irish trailed not only most Americans but also other immigrant groups that didn't come close to matching the political influence of the Irish. In fact, among all European immigrants to America, the Irish rose the slowest economically, and it wasn't until the decline of those political machines that a substantial Irish middle class began to emerge.[1]

Likewise among blacks, political and economic success historically have not moved in lockstep. Following the Civil War, "politics emerged as the principal focus of black aspirations," writes historian Eric Foner in his history of Reconstruction.[2] "Although whites generally retained political control, the fact that well over six hundred blacks, the majority former slaves, served as legislators represented a stunning change in American politics."[3] A small number of these pathbreaking elected officials improved their own financial lot but not necessarily that of their black constituents. "Although some black politicians achieved bourgeois status and others aspired to it, few successfully translated political power into a share of economic growth of their states." Foner writes: "Indeed, for many blacks, political involvement led not to social mobility but to devastating loss."[4]

Some 100 years later, following passage of the Civil Rights Act of 1964 and the Voting Rights Act of 1965, black leaders would begin another major push for political power to help remedy social inequality. Between 1970 and 2010, the number of black elected officials climbed from fewer than 1,500 to more than 10,000.[5] The list would include black mayors of major U.S. cities, black state legislators, black governors, black members of Congress, and, of course, Barack Obama, the first black president. Those decades happened to coincide with a major expansion of the welfare state initiated by

Lyndon Johnson's Great Society programs and continued by his successor, Richard Nixon. Yet this period also featured slower black progress in some areas, and outright retrogression in others. In the wake of the War on Poverty, black labor force participation declined, black unemployment rates rose, and the black nuclear family disintegrated. Between 1960 and 1995, the proportion of black children living with both parents fell from two-thirds to one-third.[6]

It turns out that the most significant progress among blacks has coincided neither with greater political representation nor with massive welfare-state interventions. Rather, blacks have tended to do better when the country's economy is doing better and they have had access to labor markets. What's needed more than political saviors, racial preferences, and wealth-redistribution schemes is economic growth and opportunity. "The greatest twenty-five years of black progress after Emancipation itself came between the early postwar period and around 1973," writes Ohio University labor economist Richard Vedder. "The real median income of the black population more than doubled between 1948 and 1973, increasing an astonishing 3 percent per year. If average instead of medians are used to calculate real income, the increase was even larger."[7]

Another recent analysis of black social mobility in the twentieth century reaches a similar conclusion. The "progress toward equality for black Americans didn't begin in 1965," write Harvard political scientist Robert Putnam and his co-author, Shaylyn Romney Garrett, in their 2020 book, *The Upswing*. "By many measures, blacks were moving toward parity with whites well before the victories of the Civil Rights revolution, despite the limitations imposed by Jim Crow." Moreover, "*after* the Civil Rights movement, that longstanding trend toward racial equality slowed, stopped, and even reversed."[8] The emphasis is the authors'. "Overall, African American incomes rose relative to white incomes for the first two-thirds of the century," they add, and "most scholars agree that income levels by race converged at the greatest rate between 1940 and 1970."[9]

In 2016, Barack Obama saw his preferred successor, Hillary Clinton, go down in shocking defeat to Donald Trump. Not only did blacks lose substantial political clout, but the new president was presented in the mainstream media as a racist whose policies would harm the interests of racial and ethnic minorities. Yet over the next three years, blacks and Hispanics experienced record-low rates of unemployment and poverty, and wages for workers at the bottom rose faster than they did for management. Prior to the global pandemic, black Americans were significantly better off economically under Trump than they'd ever been under Obama.

Whether that was the goal of the Trump administration, or an unintended consequence, is outside the purview of this slim volume. You will not find a psychoanalysis of the former president by me in the essay that follows. I did not vote for Trump in 2016 or in 2020. My newspaper columns and television commentary regularly took the administration to task for its immigration restrictionism and trade protectionism. Nor did Trump's derogatory comments about women and minorities, his marble-mouthed responses to white nationalists, and his behavior on January 6, 2021, when his supporters ransacked the Capital, escape my criticism.[10]

Nevertheless, this book was not written to score partisan political points. Rather, its purpose is to tell an underreported story about black economic advancement in the pre-pandemic economy, why it happened, and which kinds of public policies facilitated it. Most of the media could not see past Trump's Twitter feed and serial norm-breaking. That was perhaps understandable on some level, but it's no excuse for wholesale abandonment of fairness and objectivity. The reality is that racial inequality improved on Trump's watch, and much of the media were too busy agitating against him to take note or give credit where it was due. Reporters suspended any professional and ethical standards in a concerted effort to take down a president they didn't like. In some respects, their behavior was no less reckless than Donald Trump's.

≥≤

THIS BOOK WOULD NEVER have come to fruition without the interest and guidance of Susan Arellano, publisher of Templeton Press. I also thank the Thomas W. Smith Foundation, the Searle Freedom Trust, the Bader Family Foundation, the

Gale Foundation, and the Manhattan Institute, where I have been a senior fellow since 2016, for their continued support of my work. Stuart Anderson of the National Foundation for Policy Research and Alex Nowrasteh of the Cato Institute read early drafts of parts of the manuscript, and I thank them for their insights. Conversations with Michael Strain, Michael Saltsman, David Neumark, Brian Riedl, Douglas Holtz-Eakin, Richard Burkhauser, Scott Winship, Kevin Corinth, and Mike Solon gave me a better understanding of the history and the data, though the conclusions are my own. And Brandon McCoy's research assistance was invaluable. Finally, I thank my wife, Naomi, and our children for their love and inspiration.

PART I

> ≶

The Black Boom

CHAPTER 1

Black Progress: Trump vs. Obama

><

A FEW MONTHS AFTER Joe Biden took office, the *New York Times* published a column by David Brooks about Donald Trump supporters and how they were responding to the young Biden presidency. According to Brooks, there were "increasing signs that the Trumpian base is radicalizing" and that Republican voters were exhibiting "apocalyptic pessimism" regarding the new administration. "What's happening can only be called a venomous panic attack," he wrote. "Since the election, large swaths of the Trumpian right have decided America is facing a crisis like never before and they are the small army of warriors fighting with Alamo-level desperation to ensure the survival of the country as they conceive it."[1] Though Brooks never says so in the column, these reactions were every bit as applicable to the political left's end-is-nigh rhetoric surrounding the election of Trump four years earlier. Less than two weeks after Trump took office, one commentator even claimed that his presidency posed an "existential" danger to America. That commentator's name was David Brooks.[2]

If Brooks's take on Trump loyalists displayed a stunning lack of self-awareness, his own "apocalyptic pessimism" regarding Trump's 2016 victory over Hillary Clinton was hardly unique among media elites. *Slate* magazine said that Trump's win revealed "our unjust, racist, sexist country for what it is."[3] The *New Yorker* magazine wrote that the outcome was "nothing less than a tragedy for the American republic, a tragedy for the Constitution, and a triumph for the forces, at home and abroad, of nativism, authoritarianism, misogyny, and racism."[4] The reason why such feverish reactions to Trump's election are worth revisiting at the outset of this short volume is because they went on to inform media coverage of his presidency from start to finish. During the 2016 campaign, influential news organs that already tended to lean left politically became more openly ideological and oppositional in their White House *reporting*, not just on their editorial pages. In February 2017, the *Washington Post* added the slogan "Democracy Dies in Darkness" below its masthead to convey, according to the paper's spokesperson, "who we are to the many millions of readers who have come to us for the first time over the last year."[5]

The *New York Times* went even further in discarding any pretense of objectivity in its coverage of Trump. An August 2016 front-page story by the paper's media reporter, Jim Rutenberg, said that it was necessary for his colleagues to "move closer than you've ever been to being oppositional" when writing about the Trump campaign. "If you're a working journalist and you believe that Donald J. Trump is a demagogue playing to the nation's worst racist and nationalistic tendencies," wrote Rutenberg, "you have to throw out the textbook American journalism has been using for the better part of the past half-century."[6] Moreover, this move to suspend professional standards was enthusiastically applauded by self-styled guardians of journalistic ethics. Writing in a 2016 edition of the *Columbia Journalism Review*, a leading industry publication, media studies professor David Mindich offered his imprimatur to political journalists who were abandoning "the practice of steadfast detachment" in favor of "pushing explicitly against" Trump's White House bid. Around the same time, a journalism professor at New York University wrote in the *Washington Post* that reporters must "do things they have never done." Specifically, he instructed, they must "call Trump out with a forcefulness unseen before" and "explain to the public that Trump is a special case, and the normal rules do not apply."[7] The Washington press corps largely obliged the professor, but Trump won the election anyway, which not only annoyed, but confused and even angered, a media establishment that had spent the previous year telling the public that Hillary Clinton would win easily.

The problem was not that the prognosticators called it the wrong way. The consensus view at the time, which I shared, was that Trump would be rejected by an electorate who saw him as unsuitable for the presidency. I predicted that Trump's inexperience and character flaws—his repugnant birtherism and his disparaging remarks about women and immigrants—would prove fatal to his campaign. I was wrong. Perhaps not surprisingly in hindsight, the sensibilities and priorities of political journalists based in places like Washington and New York turned out to be quite different from those of Middle America. But upsets are not unheard of in politics, and Trump was an unconventional candidate who pulled a genuine upset. The problem was how the media responded to his victory. Having failed to anticipate the outcome, journalists proceeded to actively resist it, and then spent four years willfully misinterpreting the reasons it happened. The narrative that gained the greatest currency among the elite media was that Trump's political rise was evidence of racial retrenchment. "Trump opponents take his racism for granted," wrote Martin Gurri in a long, astute essay that recounted the former president's media coverage. "[H]e stands accused of appealing to the worst instincts of the American public, and those who wish to debate the point immediately fall under suspicion of being racist themselves. The dilemma, therefore, was not *whether* Trump was racist (that was a fact) or *why* he flaunted racist views (he was a dangerous demagogue), but rather, *how* to report on his racism under the strictures of commercial journalism. Once objectivity was sacrificed, an immense field of subjective possibilities presented themselves."[8]

Reporters insisted that a surge of white bigotry had put Trump in the Oval Office and that his victory over Clinton proved beyond any doubt that racism, sexism, and xenophobia in America were ascendant. This view prevailed even though numbers-crunchers—at the *New York Times* and elsewhere—had pointed to empirical evidence that called it into serious question. For example, Trump won a smaller share of the white vote—and a larger share of blacks, Hispanics, and Asians—than Mitt Romney had won four years earlier. He also carried a majority of white women, even though he ran against one.[9] And then there was the matter of which tranche of voters most likely put Trump over the top. It turns out that they were the very same people, in battleground states like Michigan, Wisconsin, and Pennsylvania, who had voted for Barack Obama in 2008 and 2012. "It's clear that large numbers of white, working-class voters shifted from the Democrats to Mr. Trump," reads a *New York Times* analysis from 2017. "He flipped millions of white working-class Obama supporters to his side. The voter file data makes it impossible to avoid this conclusion."[10] It's certainly possible that millions of white nationalists had spent the previous eight years hiding out in the Democratic Party and throwing their support behind the first black president, but it's not very plausible.

Nonetheless, this is the narrative that drove four years of Trump media coverage and is a major reason why the Trump economy, which benefited low-income minorities more than anyone, didn't receive nearly the amount of credit it deserved. What's more, this narrative—that Donald Trump ushered in a new era of white supremacy in the United States—became so entrenched that it persisted even after Trump significantly increased his level of minority support in his losing bid for a second presidential term. In 2020, Trump saw a dip in support among whites and an uptick in support among black, Asian, and Hispanic voters. The black increase is less impressive when put into context but still notable. Between 1976 and 2004, Republican presidential candidates averaged around 11 percent of the black vote. John McCain won just 4 percent in 2008 and Mitt Romney 6 percent in 2012, but they ran against Barack Obama. In 2016, Trump, who didn't have that excuse, managed only 8 percent support among blacks, which was an improvement but still below the pre-Obama norm. Trump's 4-point increase among blacks in 2020—which included a remarkable 6-point increase among black men—got the GOP back to its traditional share of the black vote in recent decades, even while the president was regularly portrayed as a racist in the press.[11]

Trump's performance in 2020 among Latinos, which jumped to 32 percent from 28 percent, is more remarkable because it expanded well beyond the reliably Republican Cuban American voters in Florida. There, Latino support overall for Trump grew by 12 points to 47 percent, and among Puerto Ricans, who generally lean much more heavily Democratic than Cubans, he won 30 percent. But he was likewise competitive among Hispanic voters of Mexican and Central American descent in places like Arizona, Nevada, and South Texas. In 2016, Starr County, Texas, which abuts the border with Mexico, went for Clinton by a 60-point margin. Biden won it four years later by just 5 points.[12]

Regardless, the growth in support for Trump among these racial and ethnic groups during his second White House bid had little impact on the prevailing view in the press that the former president made common cause with fascists and that his policies were harmful to minorities.[13] Instead, the uptick was downplayed or ignored. And when it was acknowledged at all, it was often treated with something closer to befuddlement or disbelief. A journalist for *New York* magazine, for example, attributed Trump's improved performance among minorities in 2020 to a Republican "disinformation" campaign. There "was a disconnect between the reality of the [Democratic] party's platform and how it was perceived," he wrote, as if black and Hispanic voters would never have pulled the lever for Trump unless they had been hoodwinked into doing so.[14] Elsewhere, there was simply shock. "Even in New York City, Trump's Support Grew in Many Communities," read a December 2020 headline in the *New York Times.* "Trump's Surprising Multiracial Appeal," read another headline the same month in the *Christian Science Monitor.*

Yet none of this was surprising to anyone not taking their cues from social media or MSNBC. Following Trump's victory, two academics—historian Stephanie Muravchik and political scientist Jon A. Shields—conducted an ethnographic study of long-time Democratic strongholds that went Republican in 2016. One of the places they visited was Ottumwa, Iowa, a Rust Belt town that had consistently voted Democrat for president since 1972. Another was Elliott County, Kentucky, a small rural community in Appalachia that had never voted Republican since it was formed in the 1860s and where the ratio of registered Democrats to Republicans approximated San Francisco's. The resulting book was titled *Trump's Democrats,* and it was motivated, according to the authors, by dissatisfaction at how the mainstream media depicted Trump voters:

"We are struck . . . by the fact that the dominant explanations of Trump's appeal all have one thing in common: they all assume that something must be seriously wrong with Trump enthusiast[s]," write Muravchik and Shields. "Trump won, we are told, either because of racial prejudices or economic distress or various diseases of social despair, such as drug abuse, family breakdown and suicide. Thus, in these accounts, Trump voters are driven by anger or desperation. How else could one cast a vote for Trump. Though it is never stated explicitly, such views rest on the assumption that any well-adjusted, healthy, flourishing citizen would reject Trump."[15]

The authors had not themselves supported Trump but they showed respect for people who had, and they offer a mostly objective perspective on these voters that avoids the typical liberal condescension that was so prevalent among Washington reporters. The book posits, with mounds of reporting and data to back it up, that geographic and cultural isolation may explain why these white working-class Trump supporters had so thoroughly flummoxed the pollsters and the press. Despite Trump's wealth, these voters saw him as someone with working-class sensibilities. He was a non-ideological, transactional, you-scratch-my-back-I'll-scratch-yours politician. He was a counterpuncher who refused to let even small slights go unaddressed. He surrounded himself in office with family and friends and valued loyalty above all else. Ultimately, in their estimation, Donald Trump was a kind of old-school machine Democrat. And while he was a serial violator of coastal-elite norms, he was someone who behaved like the politicians they had encountered day-in and day-out for decades. In an interview given shortly before the 2020 election, Shields predicted that these Trump Democrats would remain loyal to the president. He was correct. Trump not only held on to them but increased their numbers. And while there weren't enough of them to deliver Trump a second term, more attentive Democrats understood that there were too many of them to ignore.

David Shor, a data scientist and Democratic strategist who analyzed the 2020 election, said it was very likely that the party's focus on progressive policies had cost it votes among blacks, Hispanics, and Asians, as well as working-class

whites. "In the summer [of 2020], following the emergence
of 'defund the police' as a nationally salient issue, support
for Biden among Hispanic voters declined," Shor said. "The
decline that we saw was very large. Nine percent or so nationwide, up to 14 or 15 percent in Florida. Roughly one in
10 Hispanic voters switched their vote from Clinton to
Trump." Shor allowed that Hispanic voters "are more liberal
on immigration than white voters," but said that "the extent
to which Hispanic voters have liberal views on immigration
is exaggerated." Democrats who assumed that decriminal-
izing illegal border crossings was supported by most Hispanics, for example, were mistaken. "In test after test that
we've done with Hispanic voters, talking about immigration
commonly sparks backlash."[16]

Shor's take on black voting patterns was equally reveal-
ing. Since 2016, white liberals have become a much larger
share of the Democratic Party. Because whites tend to be more
highly educated, and because better-educated people "tend to
have more ideologically coherent and extreme views" than
the working class, the party's moderates have had less influence. The political left tends to take the liberalness of blacks
as a given, and in 2020 that proved costly to Democrats.
"Roughly the same proportion of African American, Hispanic and white voters identify as conservative," said Shor.

So as Democrats have traded non-college-educated voters
for college-educated ones, white liberals' share of voice

and clout in the Democratic Party has gone up. And since white voters are sorting on ideology more than nonwhite voters, we've ended up in a situation where white liberals are more left wing than black and Hispanic Democrats on pretty much every issue: taxes, health care, policing, and even on racial issues or various measures of "racial resentment." So as white liberals increasingly define the party's image and messaging, that's going to turn off nonwhite conservative Democrats and push them against us.[17]

None of this is to suggest that blacks and Hispanics are poised to flee the Democratic Party in droves. Biden won the nonwhite vote handily, and Democrats are expected to continue doing so for the foreseeable future. But it does suggest that the elite media perception of Donald Trump as a force of untrammeled malevolence was not shared by millions of minority and working-class white voters who pulled the lever for him in 2016, and then did so in even greater numbers four years later. To insist that they were confused or tricked ignores a far simpler and more likely explanation: Many of these voters found themselves better off economically under Donald Trump than they had been under his predecessor.

≥≤

THE GREAT RECESSION didn't begin on Barack Obama's watch. He inherited it, along with a financial crisis, from

George W. Bush, and it was easily the worst economic downturn since the Great Depression of the 1930s. Technically, however, the recession ended during Obama's first year in office. What was remarkable was the subsequent length and persistent weakness of the recovery, both of which ran counter to prior trends.

As an economics reporter writing in 2016 explained:

> The data, which measured how Americans were doing six years into the economic recovery, show that incomes in the middle, measured in 2015 dollars, were still 1.6 percent below the previous peak of $57,423 a household, which was attained in 2007, just before the economy sank into what has come to be known as the Great Recession.
>
> How does that look compared to the nation's recent history? After the economy slipped into recession in 1969, it took only three years for incomes in the middle to rebound and surpass their previous peak. After the downturn of 1973, it took five; after back-to-back recessions in 1981 and 1982, it took seven.[18]

Some blamed the tepid recovery on the fact that the downturn had overlapped with a subprime mortgage crisis in the housing market—a sort of economic double whammy—but that's not unprecedented. "The Obama administration and some economists argue that the recovery since the Great Recession ended in 2009 has been unusually weak because of the recession's severity and the fact that it was accompanied by a major financial crisis," wrote Harvard economist Robert Barro in 2016. "Yet in a recent study of economic downturns in the U.S. and elsewhere since 1870, economist Tao Jin and I found that historically the opposite has been true. Empirically, the growth rate during a recovery relates positively to the magnitude of decline during the downturn."[19] According to Barro:

Arguing that the recovery has been weak because the downturn was severe or coincided with a major financial crisis conflicts with the evidence, which shows that a larger decline predicts a stronger recovery. Moreover, many of the biggest downturns featured financial crises. For example, the US per capita GDP growth rate from 1933–40 was 6.5% per year, the highest of any peacetime interval of several years, despite the 1937 recession. This strong recovery followed the cumulative decline in the level of per capita GDP by around 29% from 1929 to 1933 during the Great Depression.[20]

The pattern has been, historically, that the deeper the recession, the more robust the recovery. Yet that's not what we saw under the Obama administration, particularly if you were someone black or less-educated. Among people with a bachelor's degree or higher, unemployment during the Great Recession never rose above 5 percent. But for those with only some college, it reached 8.9 percent. For individuals who had obtained only a high school degree, it reached 11 percent.

And among people with less than a high school diploma, the jobless rate peaked at 15.8 percent.[21] Because blacks are overrepresented among people without a college education, the snail's-pace recovery under Obama was especially devastating for them.

When Obama began his first term, in 2009, the jobless rate was 12.7 percent for blacks and 7.8 percent for whites. At the start of his second term, in 2013, black unemployment had climbed to 13.7 percent for blacks while remaining essentially unchanged for whites, which means that black joblessness had not only worsened in absolute terms but also relative to white joblessness. In fact, during Obama's two presidential terms the unemployment rate, which *never reached* double digits for whites, *did not fall below* double digits for blacks until March 2015, the third month of his seventh year in office.[22] Nor was employment the only area where blacks were forced to be more patient. Between 2009 and 2015, income inequality expanded. Median household incomes rose by 4.4 percent for whites but only by 2.3 percent for blacks. Not until 2015 and 2016 did black median household incomes finally begin to accelerate, growing at more than double the rate—5.6 percent versus 2 percent—of white median incomes.[23] Obama's record regarding black poverty and homeownership was equally unimpressive. In 2009, the black poverty rate was 2.7 times higher than the white rate. By the end of 2016, that differential had shrunk to 2.5.[24] Over the same period, the black-white gap in homeownership widened, falling by almost 10 percent among blacks but by less than 4 percent among whites.[25]

When Trump entered the Oval Office in 2017, you can be certain that memories of all this economic hardship were still quite fresh in the minds of many blacks. Under Obama, black unemployment had reached levels unseen in more than a quarter-century.[26] Among black men, it had climbed to more than 19 percent, or nearly one in five, which hadn't happened since 1983.[27] And the labor force participation rate, which measures the share of the working-age population that is either employed or actively looking for a job, dropped to a thirty-two-year low among blacks.[28] "Things have improved from the dark days of the recession," reported the National Urban League, a black civil rights organization, shortly after Obama left office. "But the recovery for African Americans has not been as fast or as deep as it's been for whites."[29] Black political support for Obama never really waned. He won 95 percent of the black vote in 2008 and 93 percent four years later. But as a *Los Angeles Times* report on his legacy explained, "Polls have shown black people to be more satisfied with Obama the man and less with their progress under Obama the president."[30]

≥≤

PRIOR TO THE Covid-19 pandemic of 2020, the economic fortunes of blacks improved under Trump to an extent that was not only unseen under Obama but unseen going back several generations. Black unemployment and poverty reached historic lows, and black wages increased at a faster clip than white wages. One question this raises is how much credit belongs to the Trump administration, and how much credit should go to the Obama administration. Were these black gains set in motion under Obama and destined to occur no matter who succeeded him? Or do the polices that were pursued by Trump offer a more plausible explanation for what happened on his watch?

The answer is probably unknowable with any real precision because the actions of a president or an administration have only a limited effect on inflation, GDP, employment, and so forth in an economy the size of America's. Business cycles occur naturally under free-market capitalism. Their impact can be limited in severity, but no one has figured out how to eliminate them altogether. Presidents can't simply order an economic boom the same way that they can order a military strike. But even if the media tends to overly credit, or overly blame, the occupant of the White House for the state of the economy at a given time, the words and actions of an administration do impact the choices of individuals and businesses. Government can create incentives and disincentives that matter immensely.

Assessing the performance of blacks under Trump prior to the 2020 pandemic is necessarily part of a broader discussion about how all groups fared economically over the same span of time. Well into the Trump presidency, Obama continued to take credit for the strengthening economy. "By the time I left office, wages were rising, uninsurance rate was falling, poverty was falling, and that's what I handed off to the next guy," he told an audience in the fall of 2018. "So, when you hear all this talk about economic miracles right now, remember who started it."[31] Throughout his presidential campaign, Joe Biden likewise argued that robust economic growth had been bequeathed to Obama's successor. "Trump inherited the longest economic expansion in history from the Obama-Biden administration, but like everything else he's inherited, he has squandered it," Biden told Bloomberg News in June of 2020. He added that Trump had "turned his back on the middle class" by focusing on tax cuts for corporations and the wealthy.[32] Right up until the Covid-induced contraction, Democrats never stopped claiming credit for any economic good news.

Obama and Biden's arguments were obviously self-serving, but the more interesting question is whether the available evidence backs them up. It's true that the unemployment rate fell by 5.2 percentage points, from 9.9 percent to 4.7 percent, between the end of 2009 and the end of 2016.[33] It's also true that over the same eight-year period, median household income grew by $3,440, from $59,458 to $62,898.[34] And, yes, between 2017 and 2019, these trends continued. However, simply noting that unemployment already was falling, and incomes already rising, when Trump took office understates the significance of what happened over the next three years on his watch. The reality is that these trends not only continued but accelerated and did so despite the expectations at the time.

By the end of 2016, the consensus view emanating from officials at the Treasury Department, the Federal Reserve, and the Congressional Budget Office (CBO) was that the economy had essentially reached full employment and couldn't grow any faster. Despite the claims by Obama and Biden that everything was already headed in the right direction economically when Trump became president, that's simply not true. During Obama's final year in office, 2016, economic growth slipped to just 1.6 percent from 3.1 percent in 2015.[35] Put another way, the rate at which the economy had been expanding was cut nearly in half over a one-year period. Trump inherited a US economy that was slowing down, and there was widespread concern about the possibility of another recession. Lawrence Summers, who served as treasury secretary under President Bill Clinton and was a top economic advisor to President Obama, said that there was a 60 percent chance that the economy would dip into recession within a year.[36] For the years 2017, 2018, and 2019, the Fed had projected that unemployment would hover between 4.4 percent and 4.9 percent and wouldn't fall below 4.1, and that economic growth would remain between 1.7 percent and 2.2 percent.[37] The rationale, laid out in a subsequent CBO analysis, was that labor markets couldn't get any tighter than they were already without triggering inflation. "CBO projects that . . . employment will increase more slowly over the next few years than it has recently—by an average of about 160,000 jobs per month in the first half of 2017, 116,000 jobs per month in the second half of 2017, and 94,000 jobs per month in 2018," the agency wrote in a February 2017 report. "One reason that employment growth is projected to slow is that as the employment shortfall shrinks, fewer people without jobs will be available to enter employment."[38] Expectations regarding labor force participation were similarly dour. "CBO expects the labor force participation rate to average 62.8 percent this year and next year," said the agency. "The rate was also 62.8 percent last year [in 2016], roughly where it has stood, on average, since 2014." After 2018, the CBO expected labor force participation to fall, citing the retirement of large numbers of Baby Boomers as well as "lingering effects of the 2007–2009 recession and ensuing weak recovery."[39]

Similarly, the academic and media forecasts were that the next president would inherit a long recovery that had run out of steam, and thus it was time to brace for a downturn. Mark Zandi of Moody's Analytics was the lead author of a June 2016 paper that predicted "the economy will be significantly weaker if Mr. Trump's economic proposals are adopted" and that the United States would suffer "a lengthy recession" as a result. The biggest beneficiaries of Trump's proposals "are high-income households," the paper continued. "Everyone receives a tax cut under his proposals, but the bulk of the cuts would go to those at the very top of the income distribution, and the job losses resulting from his other policies would likely hit lower- and middle-income households the hardest."[40]

On the eve of the 2016 election, a Massachusetts Institute of Technology professor and former chief economist of the International Monetary Fund (IMF) wrote that "growth and employment around the world look fragile" and that "a big adverse surprise—like the election of Donald Trump in the US—would likely cause the stock market to crash and plunge the world into recession."[41] Trump "faces a ticking clock in terms of the ongoing economic recovery's life," warned a *USA Today* article just weeks after the election. "The economic expansion period the U.S. is in now is 89 months old making it the fourth longest expansion of the 21 since 1902 and twice the length of the median expansion."[42] And *New York Times* columnist Paul Krugman said the markets would "never" recover from Trump's victory and that "we are very probably looking at a global recession, with no end in sight."[43]

Brian Riedl, a tax and budget analyst at the Manhattan Institute, said that this is the context in which Trump's achievements are best assessed. "People say Trump just created the same number of jobs in 2017 and 2018 as Obama had, but when Trump took office the unemployment rate was around 4.5 percent, which means we'd pretty much run out of unemployed people," he said in an interview. "It's a lot easier to create 2 million jobs when you start out with

8 million unemployed. Trump was starting out with full employment. He created twice as many jobs as the [Congressional Budget Office] had forecast, and the economy created $1.1 trillion in more wealth than CBO had forecast because everyone assumed we had peaked, that we'd run out of capacity for more growth." Riedl added that when people assume all of this was merely a continuation of something that began under Obama, "they're assuming that there's no such thing as a business cycle, that if you create 3 million jobs one year, you should do it every year."[44] Casey Mulligan, who served as chief economist for the Council of Economic Advisors under Trump, was even more blunt: "After it became plain that experts were too pessimistic with their 2017 and 2018 forecasts, they switched to saying that economic growth was 'merely continuing the trend of the Obama economy,'" he wrote. "If following an earlier trend is such an easy accomplishment, why wasn't it predicted then? Sadly, they still have their facts wrong. The 2019 *Economic Report of the President* shows how economic indicators such as wages for low-skill workers or investment have been rising *above* the earlier trend. Something special happened in early 2017 that continues to surprise the experts."[45]

≳≲

WHAT HAPPENED in early 2017 was that the new president set about implementing what he had promised during the campaign: lower taxes and lighter regulation to spur economic growth. He nominated Kevin Hassett, who had published research showing how corporate taxes depress wages for manufacturing workers, to lead the Council of Economic Advisors.[46] And he urged Congress to pass legislation that would reduce the country's corporate rate, which was one of the highest in the developed world. "There is a long and legitimate debate about who pays corporate taxes," explained the *Wall Street Journal*. "Corporations essentially collect taxes that are ultimately paid by someone else: a combination of workers in lower wages, customers in higher prices, or shareholders in lower after-tax returns." The paper noted that the conventional wisdom, which held that the biggest burden was on shareholders, had changed in recent decades as new research on the mobility of capital in a global economy came to light. "While labor is relatively immobile, especially across national borders, capital can go wherever it wants with relative ease," the *Journal* noted. "U.S. companies have taken advantage of this reality by investing more abroad in lower-tax countries. The benefits accrue to Irish or Singaporean workers whose jobs are created by that capital investment."[47]

Trump proposed lowering the corporate tax rate in hopes that more capital would flow back home and be invested here in the United States rather than abroad. The plan was criticized by political opponents as a sop to the rich, yet mainstream economists of all stripes have long recognized that corporate tax cuts are also a boon for employees. "Some may worry that a cut in corporate taxes would benefit only the firms' wealthy owners," wrote N. Gregory Mankiw, a Harvard economist who advised President George W. Bush. "But that's not true, especially in the long run. Over time, lower corporate taxes would attract more investment in the corporate sector, increasing workers' productivity and thus their wages." Mankiw added that economists continue to debate the *size* of those wage gains but "most agree that wages would increase and that the effect would grow over time."[48]

Moreover, the very same critics of corporate tax cuts during the Trump administration—including Obama economic advisers Larry Summers and Jason Furman—had supported them during Obama's presidency. The flip-flopping extended to Democratic leaders in Congress, explained Mulligan and Tomas Philipson in a co-authored 2017 op-ed. "Suddenly, an idea that has been accepted by economists and by policy makers on both sides of the political aisle—that high taxes on businesses hurt investment, workers and the economy—is considered 'absurd,'" they wrote. "In 2015, Democrat Chuck Schumer and Republican Rob Portman co-sponsored a Senate bill to reduce the top corporate tax rate, which was the highest of any of the 35 countries in the Organization for Economic Corporation and Development. 'Our international tax system,' Mr. Schumer argued back then, 'creates incentives to send jobs and stash profits overseas, rather than creating jobs and economic growth here in the United States.'"[49] Nevertheless, top Democrats and liberal economists were committed to resisting

Trump's tax policies, even if that meant opposing what they had supported just two years earlier, and even if it harmed the very constituents—low-income minorities and working-class whites, for example—whom they claimed to care about most.

Along with the push for tax reform, Trump also moved to reduce regulations that he argued were weighing on economic growth. So-called major regulations are defined as those that impose a cost of $100 million or more on the private sector, and they exploded under President Obama. According to one analysis, the Obama administration imposed a record-breaking 600 major regulations in seven-and-a-half years, which was 20 percent more than the previous administration had imposed in 8 years.[50] On Obama's way out of the White House, in the period between Election Day in November 2016 and the beginning of the Trump presidency in January 2017, his administration issued 33 additional regulations with total costs exceeding $100 million. They included new efficiency standards for manufacturers of air conditioners ($12.3 billion) and ceiling fans (4.4 billion), and new requirements for commercial vehicle operators ($3.6 billion).[51] These regulatory burdens affect hiring and pay and are one reason why the economic recovery under Obama was so tepid. As one industry newsletter explained in a 2016 report, "regulations have contributed to a 30 percent decline in overall employment in the heating, ventilation, air conditioning and refrigeration (HVACR) and water heating industries since 2001." The Obama Department of Energy even acknowledged that its regulatory agenda could hurt small business owners. At the extreme, compliance costs could even determine whether an enterprise remains a going concern or must shut down operations. "It is possible that the small manufacturers will choose to leave the industry," DOE stated in a 2014 rule making for commercial air conditioners.[52]

When you're imposing major regulations at a rate of more than one per day for 8 straight years, "that's a pretty significant headwind," Douglas Holtz-Eakin, a former director of the Congressional Budget Office under George W. Bush, told me. "Trump comes in, and in his first year—from inauguration until September 30th—there are $5 billion in regulatory costs. Not $100 billion but $5 billion. And in year two, it's negative $15 billion, or something like that. In year three, it's still negative but less so."[53] A Cato Institute analysis of regulatory activity in the first two years of the Obama and Trump administrations counted a total of 6,793 new rule makings for Obama and 4,310, or 36 percent fewer, for Trump. More significantly, among major regulations, the tally was 176 for Obama and only 90, or just over half as many, for Trump.[54] "For the private sector, and the small-business community in particular, it was like night and day," said Holtz-Eakin. "Small-business optimism jumped and the climate for growth and hiring people was tremendous." He continued:

The economy had reached a low point in the second quarter of 2016, and it grew faster every quarter consecutively until the third quarter of 2018, when Trump picked a trade war with China. It still grew pretty fast after that, but it slowed down somewhat. At a time when population growth and the labor force participation rate should have been creating something like 80,000 to 95,000 jobs a month, we kept getting jobs reports of 230,000, 235,000. I was the one saying this can't continue. It was astonishing. That economy pulled people into the labor force and put people to work who had been disconnected from the economic life of the country for a long, long time. One of the best things that ever happened.[55]

Trump's often indefensible behavior and nonstop Twitter rants commanded most of the media's attention during his presidency, and how could they not? Voters expect a certain decorum from the president, and so Trump himself must share a lot of the blame for the fact that his economic record isn't better known and appreciated. Still, the record is what it is, and far too many crusading journalists chose to indulge their political biases instead of simply reporting the facts. Trump's theatrics notwithstanding, he pursued the tax and regulatory agenda of a typical conservative Republican politician, and on his watch tens of millions of Americans who had been struggling economically for decades saw meaningful improvement in their lives, including many members of low-income minority groups.

≥≤

THE TAX CUT AND JOBS ACT was passed in December 2017. Although what followed won't settle the debate over whether labor or capital benefits most from a reduction in corporate taxes, it ought to at least inform the conversation. The corporate rate fell from 35 percent to 21 percent, and, in addition, companies were given an opportunity to "repatriate" cash being held overseas at a tax rate of just 15.5 percent. Taxes on wages and investment also fell. It was the most significant tax code reform in 30 years, and the dividends were almost immediate. By the end of January 2018, more than 260 businesses—including major employers such as Walmart, FedEx, and 3M Company— had announced wage and salary increases, bonuses, and 401(k) match increases going to at least 3 million workers because of the new law.[56] Exxon Mobil announced that it planned to invest an addition $35 billion in the United States over the next five years. "These investments are underpinned by the unique strengths of our company and enhanced by the historic tax reform recently signed into law," said Exxon's CEO. "These positive developments will mean more jobs and economic expansion across the United States in a myriad of industries."[57]

Gross domestic product, which had declined to 1.6 percent in 2016, climbed to 2.2 percent in 2017 and to 2.9 percent in 2018. As remarkable was the change in gross private domestic investment, which is a measure of how much money domestic businesses invest within their own country. It had *declined* by 1.3 percent in 2016, but grew by 4.8 percent in 2017 and by another 6 percent in 2018. Lower taxes and lighter regulations were intended to spur economic growth, and business responded accordingly. Part of what made the Trump boom unique, however, is who benefited the most. While an overwhelming majority of Americans found themselves better off than they had been under Obama, the gains were not equally distributed. Instead, the economy grew in ways that mostly benefited low-income individuals and the middle class, categories that cover a disproportionate number of blacks. In 2016, the percentage of blacks who had not completed high school was nearly twice the percentage of whites—15 percent versus 8 percent—and the percentage of adults who had earned a bachelor's degree or higher was 35 percent for whites and only 21 percent for blacks.[58]

These education gaps are reflected in where blacks work and how much they earn, since our economy tends to reward educational achievement. Blacks are overrepresented in the retail, health care and transportation industries, for example, which provide tens of millions of working- and middle-class jobs. Blacks are 12 percent of the workforce, but according to the Bureau of Labor Statistics they are 18 percent of the workers in "motor vehicles and motor vehicle equipment manufacturing," 20 percent of the workers in "animal slaughtering and processing," 20 percent of the workers in "general merchandise stores, including warehouse clubs and supercenters," and 27 percent of "taxi and limousine service" workers.[59] In 2019,

54 percent of black households earned less than $50,000 per year, versus 33 percent of white households. At the other end of the income distribution, slightly more than half of all white households (50.7 percent) earned at least $75,000, compared to less than a third (29.4 percent) of black households.[60] What this means is that reductions in income inequality can translate into reductions in racial inequality, which is what the country experienced in the pre-pandemic Trump economy.

Between 2017 and 2019, median household incomes grew by 15.4 percent among blacks, while growing by only 11.5 percent among whites, and the gains were concentrated among low-income earners. A Federal Reserve report from 2020 notes that real (inflation-adjusted) median incomes between 2016 and 2019 grew by 5 percent across all demographic groups, but that families "at the top of the income and wealth distributions experienced very little, if any, growth in median and mean net worth between 2016 and 2019 after experiencing large gains between 2013 and 2016." Meanwhile, families "near the bottom of the income and wealth distributions generally continued to experience substantial gains in median and mean net worth between 2016 and 2019." The report, which is released every three years, also notes that white, affluent and college-educated households had less income growth than other groups and that "more broadly, the income gaps between families with a college degree and those without one decreased." Specifically, median income rose by 9 percent for people without a high school degree and by 6.3 percent by those who had completed high school, but it fell by 2.3 percent for those who had earned a bachelor's degree or higher.[61]

"The comparative data is striking, and mostly ignored by the press," wrote the *Wall Street Journal* in a January 2020 editorial. "During the first 11 quarters of the Trump Presidency, wages for the bottom 10% of earners over age 25 rose an average of 5.9% annually compared to 2.4% during Barack Obama's second term, according to the latest demographic data from the Bureau of Labor Statistics. Wages for the middle two quartiles increased 3.2% compared to 2.2% and 2.7 percent between 2012 and 2016." The *Journal* continued:

> Less educated workers have also seen the strongest gains. Wages have risen at a 6.1% annual clip for workers over 25 with a high school degree and 3.9% for those with some college—both about three times faster than during the second Obama term. Wage gains have also accelerated though to a lesser degree—to 3.2% from 2.2% for college grads. . . .
>
> Irony alert: Socialism-loving young people are getting the biggest pay raises. Wages have increased 5.8% annually for teens, 4.4% for 20 to 24-year-olds and 4.8% for 25 to 34-year-olds during the Trump Presidency.[62]

Political reporters were not unaware of this data. Rather, they chose to ignore or downplay it because it was inconvenient. In their view, Trump, because he was a Republican and because he was Trump, had it in for blacks, and thus his policy preferences would be harmful to minorities. To highlight the fact that significant racial disparities were narrowing on his watch—that the administration's tax and regulatory reforms were mainly boosting the working and middle classes rather than "the rich"—would have undermined a narrative that the media preferred to advance, regardless of its veracity.

≳≲

THIS WAS NOT THE FIRST TIME that the pace of black earnings exceeded those of whites. Between 1939 and 1960, annual median incomes of black men and women grew faster than those of their white counterparts.[63] Before the passage of major civil rights legislation, and at a time when racial discrimination was still legal and widespread, blacks were increasing their years of schooling relative to whites and entering middle class professions at unprecedented rates. In the 1960s and prior to the era of affirmative action, black household income grew by 100 percent while rising by just 69 percent for whites, and in less than a decade black college enrollment nearly doubled. According to census data, by 1971, "Black family heads with just a high school degree and no more had incomes 73% that of whites," but "for blacks with some college education the figure was 90% of comparable white income."[64]

Tellingly, the 1960s were also a period when the number of black female-headed households began to grow dramatically. "From 1959 to 1971, the number of black male-headed families in poverty *decreased* by more than half (54%) while the comparable number of female-headed families *increased* by 60%," demographer Ben Wattenberg reported in his 1974 book, *The Real America.* Wattenberg went on to explain the significance of this development:

> Of all black families in poverty in 1959, more than two-thirds (70%) were male headed. The balance (30%) were female-headed. But twelve years later, by 1971, there was a reversal: Almost six in ten (59%) of the black families in poverty were female headed and only four in ten (41%) were male headed.
>
> In short, there was a sexual inversion of the poverty numbers for blacks: There were more female-headed families; the male-headed families were exiting from "poverty"; the female-headed families were entering into "poverty."[65]

Liberals today are eager to link racial economic disparities to slavery, Jim Crow, and ongoing "systemic" bias. Yet census data going back more than 70 years, to a time when discrimination was far more prevalent than it is in the third decade of the twenty-first century, suggest that black family formation is a more significant factor. Not only has the poverty rate for black married couples been in the single digits since

1994, in some years it has been lower than for whites as a whole. Similarly, while labor force participation rates for black men trail those of white men and have for decades, the labor force participation rates of *married* black men are higher than the rates for white men who never married.[66] "Do racists care whether someone black is married or unmarried?" writes the economist Thomas Sowell. "If not, then why do married blacks escape poverty so much more often than other blacks, if racism is the main reason for black poverty? If the continuing effects of past evils such as slavery play a major *causal* role today, were the ancestors of today's black married couples exempt from slavery and other injustices?"[67]

Part of the explanation for this black upward *economic* mobility was simply physical mobility. Between 1915 and 1970, some 6 million blacks migrated from poorer rural areas in the South to wealthier urban environs in both the South and North. For many of them, incomes increased accordingly. Doing the exact same job paid more in Cleveland than in rural Alabama. Other factors included the labor demands created by World War II and its aftermath. By 1967 the black unemployment rate in Detroit, for instance, was just 3.4 percent, which was lower than the national average for whites.[68] As "more and more African Americans migrated, they were also better positioned to benefit from a period of unprecedented national economic growth as well as the dramatic upward wage compression that took place from 1940 to 1970," write the political scientist Robert Putnam and co-author Shaylyn

Romney Garrett in their 2020 book, *The Upswing*.[69] The "progress toward equality for black Americans didn't begin in 1965," they write. "By many measures, blacks were moving toward parity with whites well before the victories of the Civil Rights revolution, despite the limitations imposed by Jim Crow." What's more, "*after* the Civil Rights movement, that longstanding trend toward racial equality slowed, stopped and even reversed."[70] The authors add:

Overall, African American incomes rose relative to white incomes for the first two-thirds of the century. Although there is very little literature examining economic outcomes by race in the decades between 1900 and 1940, what data do exist suggest modest progress toward racial parity in income during this period. And most scholars agree that income levels by race converged at the greatest rate between 1940 and 1970.[71]

The black-white gap in high school completion "improved dramatically between the 1940s and the early 1970s, after which it slowed, never reaching parity," write Putnam and Garrett. "College completion followed the same trajectory until 1970, then sharply reversed." Similarly, the racial gap in home-ownership "steadily narrowed between 1900 and 1970, then stagnated, then reversed." After 1970, the income-gap reductions also slowed. The authors note that blacks on balance have "experienced flat or *downward* mobility in recent decades."[72]

This sort of empirical evidence is regularly ignored by those who cite the enduring effects of slavery, Jim Crow, redlining, public school segregation, and employer discrimination to explain today's racial disparities in everything from labor force participation and income to educational attainment and criminal behavior. But how is it that previous generations of blacks, who lived during the ugliest decades of Jim Crow and were much closer to the institution of slavery, were able to outperform blacks in later generations, who lived under black police chiefs, mayors, governors, senators, and a twice-elected black president? If high rates of fatherless families, teen pregnancies, substance abuse, violent crime, and other black social pathologies are a "legacy of slavery," then why were those rates significantly lower in the first hundred years after slavery than they would become in the post-sixties era, when by any objective measure systemic racism was abating and massive welfare-state interventions had been initiated?

The use of racism as a blanket explanation for economic disparities is also undermined by the fact that Asian Americans as a group out-earn whites, even though whites have experienced less discrimination in the United States historically than Asians. Furthermore, blacks out-earn Hispanics, even though few would argue that Hispanics have endured more discrimination in the U.S. than blacks. Clearly, racial and ethnic prejudice are not as determinative as many liberals claim. Cultural attitudes, behaviors, and habits would seem to play a larger role than is generally acknowledged. That so many Asians excel academically and economically has a lot to do with the fact that they are significantly more likely than other groups to have intact families. That Tiger Mom is usually married to the father of her children.[73]

≥≤

OTHERS CAN DEBATE whether Trump *set out* to narrow racial inequality. His stated goal on the campaign trail was to grow the economy to the benefit of the working class, which is what came to pass even while the media all but conspired to keep quiet about it or to credit Obama. What we can say with more certainty is that the gains of blacks prior to the pandemic were unprecedented. Yes, blacks had made strides economically during previous expansions, like the period between 1983 and 1989, when annual GDP growth averaged 4.4 percent, or from 1994 to 2000, when annual growth averaged 4 percent. Still, this time was different. Citing research conducted by Professor Robb Sinn, a mathematician at the University of North Georgia, the *Christian Science Monitor* reported that the "weekly wage for Americans in the 10th percentile of earners, of which minorities make up a greater share, grew by $4.24 per quarter in the first three years of the Trump presidency, compared with an average of 88 cents of gains per quarter across Barack Obama's eight years." And even though "higher-income groups saw weekly wages grow by larger dollar amounts, the gains in the 10th and 25th per-centiles were larger than any other group."[74]

Moreover, people already in the work force were not the only beneficiaries. According to Sinn's calculations, "the Trump economy also attracted 400,000 new Black wage-earners per year during his presidency" while "Obama aver-aged 250,000." The professor speculated that these wage gains might have contributed to Trump's bump in minority support for his re-election bid. Blue-collar workers of any race "don't need advanced statistical analysis," he told the paper. "They're, like, 'Hey, I was getting raises. I was doing better, I could take my kids to Disney.' If their finances are better, they remember that. This shows what actually happened with real blue-collar workers. It shows what was actually going on at those kitchen tables."[75]

But if those workers—or anyone else—are interested in an "advanced statistical analysis" of how the working class fared under Trump, the economists Richard V. Burkhauser, Kevin Corinth, and Douglas Holtz-Eakin have provided one. Between the fourth quarter of 2017 and the fourth quarter of 2019, "nominal weekly wages grew by 15.6 percent for work-ers at the 10th percentile of the wage distribution, outpacing nominal median weekly wage growth of 10.2 percent" for all workers, the authors write in a 2021 paper on the eco-nomic progress of the working class prior to the pandemic.[76] Broken down by racial and ethnic group, "Nominal median weekly wage growth for black workers of 12.0 percent and for Hispanic workers of 10.2 percent between 2017 Q4 and 2019 Q4 outpaced the 9.8 percent growth for white workers." This improvement to the financial well-being of historically disadvantaged groups was especially noteworthy given that blacks in recent decades have been relatively less mobile than whites. Between 2017 and 2019 the unemployment rate fell by slightly more among blacks (.7 percentage points) than it did among whites (.6 percentage points).[77] Blacks have higher disability rates than whites, and in some large metro areas it's been measured at 2.5 times higher.[78] Yet under Trump, the "economic well-being among people with disabilities increased, more so than those without disabilities, even as reliance on disability assistance programs fell." And the official poverty rate "reached record lows for all racial and ethnic groups in 2019, including falling below 20% among Black Americans for the first time on record."[79]

In response to the Great Recession, the Obama administration expanded the social safety net to help off-set earnings losses among low-wage workers. Unemployment insurance was expanded to 99 weeks in many states, for example, and work requirements for food stamps were waived even for non-disabled adults without dependents. While this response helped somewhat to mitigate the loss in household income, there were of course trade-offs. Burkhauser and his co-authors posit that the Obama approach "came with a cost—discouraging work and thus contributing to prolonged labor market weakness." The takeaway from the Great Recession "is that strong economic growth and a hot labor market do more to improve the economic well-being of the working class and historically disadvantaged groups than a slow recovery that relies on safety net policies to help replace lost earnings." Obama maintained that his safety net policies were *helping*, but the evidence shows that they were mostly *interfering*. "Thus, while a strong social safety net is vital to protect workers from negative shocks, especially during recessions, it is not a replacement for a strong economy," the authors write. "The working class including traditionally disadvantaged Americans were substantially better off in 2019 than they were during the slow post-recession recovery when the labor market was weaker and transfer programs were more generous."[80]

Donald Trump did his own share of "interfering" with market processes as well, namely through his trade and immigration protectionism, which will be discussed shortly. But on balance, his administration's focus on economic growth rather than wealth redistribution made a measurable difference in the lives of millions of working-class Americans, a disproportionate number of whom were black and brown. "Every time the Obama administration had the choice between redistributing income and increasing economic growth, they chose redistributing income," Burkhauser told me in an interview. "And there's a price to pay for that."[81] Trump lightened regulatory burdens and signed a major tax cut that unleashed what John Maynard Keynes dubbed the economy's "animal spirits." What followed, regardless of Trump's intensions, were not only broad-based increases in employment and income but also a narrowing of economic inequality. People who had been out of the labor force returned to work. People who had been working part time began working full time. And groups with the highest unemployment rate—teenagers, for example—saw more job prospects. "In 2019, growth in median income was not just to the highest level, it was the biggest gain ever," said Mike Solon, a veteran Washington budget and tax analyst. "In fact, it was 47% more than the next real median household gain ever. It was 13 times the average. This one year, 2019, was more than all 8 years of income gains under Obama. Anyone who claims that somehow this was inevitable should remember that 2016 was one of the worst years for the economy. It was recessionary."[82]

The *Economic Report of the President* is published annually by the White House Council of Economic Advisers. The last one released before the pandemic covered the performance of the economy through 2019, and it was written (justifiably) in full-brag mode, noting that "a stronger U.S. economy over the past three years has especially helped racial and ethnic minorities, less-educated individuals, people living in poverty, and those who had been out of the labor force."[83] Duly noting that the "U.S. economy is the strongest it has been in the last half-century," it adds that under the Trump administration, "and for the first time on record, there are more job openings than unemployed people."[84] The jobless rate dipped to 3.5 percent in 2019, a 50-year low, and falling unemployment "reduced the share of the population on unemployment insurance to the lowest level since recording started in 1967." Not only did black unemployment "hit the lowest level on record" but "lows have also been achieved for Asians, Hispanics, American Indians or Alaskan Natives, veterans, those without a high school degree, and persons with disabilities, among others." During the economic recovery under Obama, more than 1 million prime-age workers—individuals between 25 and 54—left the labor force and were no longer even looking for a job. The report explains that this trend reversed course under Trump:

Since the 2016 election, the economy has added more than 7 million jobs, far exceeding the 1.9 million predicted by the Congressional Budget Office in its final pre-election forecast. These gains have brought people from the sidelines into employment. In parts of 2019, nearly three-quarters of people entering employment came from out of the labor force—the highest rate on record. And the prime-age labor force is growing, reversing losses under the prior administration's expansion period. This evidence suggests that the labor market's revival over the past three years is not a continuation of past trends but instead is the result of President Trump's progrowth policies.[85]

The Trump White House was forced to tout its own achievements more often than most administrations because they were otherwise likely to go unnoticed by the Washington media establishment. Only after Trump lost his re-election bid did you begin to see, occasionally, stories in major press outlets that acknowledged the significance of his economic achievements. In January of 2021, for example, the *New York Times* ran a piece with the headline "The Most Important Thing Biden Can Learn from the Trump Economy." The story noted that under Trump, "it has become clear that the United States economy can surpass what technocrats once thought were its limits," a tacit acknowledgement that the slow-growth Obama years didn't have to be the "new normal." The "experience of this presidency—particularly the buoyant economy before the pandemic began—shows what is possible," said the paper. "It may not have been the best economy ever, as [Trump] has repeatedly claimed, but it was easily the strongest since the late-1990s, and before that you have to go back to the late 1960s to find similar conditions."[86]

Nevertheless, mainstream media acknowledgement of Trump's economic successes remains rare, and it often falls to former members of his administration to lay out simple facts. "Whereas during most of the expansion through 2016, we observed widening wage, income and wealth inequality," said Trump economic adviser Tyler Goodspeed in a conversation with fellow Trump economic adviser Kevin Hassett, "in the first three years of the Trump administration—and particularly following historic tax reform in 2017—we observed substantial declines in all three." During Trump's first three years, "real wage growth at the 10th percentile (+9.8 percent) was more than double real wage growth at the 90th percentile (+4.8 percent). Since the 2017 Tax Cuts and Jobs Act, real wealth for the bottom 50 percent of the distribution rose 28.4 percent, while that of the top 1 percent rose 8.9 percent, with the bottom 50 percent's share of real wealth rising while that of the top 1 percent declined." By the end of 2019, "real median household income was already $6,000 higher that it was in 2016."[87] This aspect of Trump's presidency was rarely if ever discussed in places like the *Washington Post* or CNN, and when it was, reporters bent over backwards trying to minimize the achievement or credit his predecessor. It wasn't just "spin." It was unprofessional, dishonest, and a disservice to voters. The former president's unconventional behavior didn't help, of course, but the job of Washington reporters is to offer fair-minded White House coverage of significant developments, even when those developments don't align with the personal political preferences of the press corps. Trump's economic accomplishments were substantive, and in some cases historic. Yet too many in the press simply refused to do their job.

≽≼

ONE TAKEAWAY FROM the Trump era is that what black upward mobility requires has less to do with racial preferences—or even with any conscientious effort on the part of a president to help blacks—and more to do with advancing policies in the service of economic freedom for everyone. Historically, black economic fortunes improved most dramatically in the aftermath of World War I and World War II, periods of tremendous growth and prosperity for the nation as a whole. The political left is eager to credit the New Deal and the Great Society with black progress, yet blacks were not only advancing more rapidly in absolute terms prior to those government interventions but also relative to white advancement. "Black people were among the major victims of the New Deal," writes the historian Jim Powell. "Large numbers of blacks were unskilled and held entry-level jobs, and when New Deal policies forced wage rates above market levels, hundreds of thousands of these jobs were destroyed."[88] During this period, black-white income gaps expanded, a situation that wouldn't reverse itself until World War II created a huge demand for workers, particularly those at the bottom of the economic ladder.

Similarly, the Lyndon Johnson Great Society programs at best continued pre-existing economic trends among blacks, and at worst retarded black progress. In 1940, 87 percent of black households were poor. By 1960, it had dropped to 47 percent, even though the landmark civil rights legislation of the 1960s had yet to be enacted and the War on Poverty had yet to be launched. Between 1940 and 1970, blacks increased their years of schooling at a faster pace than whites, and the percentage of blacks in white-collar jobs quadrupled—all before the era of affirmative action. "There was a substantial black middle-class already in existence by the end of the 1960s," write Stephan Thernstrom and Abigail Thernstrom in *America in Black and White*. "In the years since, it has continued to grow, *but not at a more rapid pace* than in the preceding three decades, despite a common impression to the contrary."[89] The emphasis is the Thernstroms', who add: "Great occupational advances were made by African Americans before preferential policies were introduced in the late 1960s. Whether that progress would have continued without a national commitment to affirmative action is open to debate. But it certainly cannot be assumed that the progress that has been made since then could not possibly have occurred without affirmative action."[90]

This history suggests that blacks need opportunities more than they need coddling or special treatment, and what a rapidly expanding economy provides are opportunities. A president who understands and appreciates the ingredients for overall economic growth is far more useful to blacks than one who just happens to share their racial classification. If the election of Barack Obama represented black political progress, and racial progress in general, the experience of his presidency demonstrated the limitations of black political clout, in and of itself, when it comes to advancing a group economically. After Trump's election in 2016, the race scholar Shelby Steele wrote, "I hope he will not be a 'redemptive' president, as his predecessor longed to be. There should be no posture of contrition, no undercurrent of apology, when he discusses social inequities."[91] Steele got his wish, and blacks saw economic progress under Trump that the Obama administration didn't come close to matching.

CHAPTER 2
The Immigration Distraction

————————— ❥❦ —————————

THE DEBATE OVER how much credit Donald Trump deserves for the economy's performance prior to the pandemic is part of a larger debate over which policies advance economic prosperity and which policies are more likely to retard it. Some conservatives have argued that immigration restrictionism is a boon for the US economy, while some liberals maintain that minimum wage increases are a major factor in reducing economic inequality. Conservatives cite Trump's relentless vocal opposition to illegal border crossings as a major factor in the economic growth that we witnessed on his watch and a primary reason why black-white disparities narrowed. Liberals argue that any income-inequality reduction we did witness between 2017 and 2020 is properly credited not to tax cuts or deregulation but to states passing laws that increased the minimum wage, something the Obama administration and political left had long advocated. Let's address these arguments in turn.

Illegal immigration was a central theme of Trump's campaign in 2016, and he talked about it seemingly nonstop as president, whether he was giving a State of the Union address or holding a rally in front of adoring crowds. Part of the reason I doubted Trump's chances was that GOP candidates going back decades who had made opposition to illegal immigration a defining issue—Pat Buchanan, Pete Wilson, Tom Tancredo—had consistently come up short. Voters might complain about immigration to pollsters but they had inevitably voted on other issues. Hence, successful Republican candidates like Ronald Reagan had referred somewhat dismissively to the "illegal alien fuss," opposed walling off the southern border with Mexico, and said Hispanics were already Republicans "who don't know it yet."[1] Both Bush presidents hewed to Reagan's thinking on immigration, and George W. Bush in particular worked to portray the party as racially and ethnically inclusive. Even GOP presidential hopefuls who were nominated but lost the general election, such as John McCain and Mitt Romney, weren't nearly as protectionist in tone as Trump, who repeatedly vowed to build a "beautiful" new border wall and make Mexico pay for it. Trump proved doubters like me wrong. He ran on opposition to illegal immigration and won both the nomination and the presidency, thus demonstrating that the issue could be a political winner for Republican presidential hopefuls. In office, he pushed for reductions to legal immigration as well, by calling for an end to the diversity visa lottery program, reducing the number of people eligible for asylum, and supporting legislation sponsored by Republican lawmakers that would have cut legal immigration by half.

Trump viewed immigrants, whether they were here legally or illegally, as economic threats. His fear was that foreign workers would displace Americans and put downward pressure on wages. It's a common concern that is older than the United States itself. By the 1750s Benjamin Franklin was already fretting about the "Importation of Foreigners into a Country that has as many Inhabitants as the present Employments and Provisions for Subsistence will bear."[2] A hundred years ago, labor leaders not only were pushing for shorter work weeks to create more jobs but also wanted tighter restrictions on immigration to prevent native-born Americans from having to vie for jobs with foreign workers.[3] California and Oregon passed laws that barred the use of Chinese laborers on public works projects. New York and Illinois went ever further, banning the use of any "alien" workers on certain construction jobs.[4]

Frederick Douglass, the celebrated black abolitionist who helped convince Abraham Lincoln to sign the Emancipation Proclamation, spoke out against restrictions on Asian immigration. "I submit that this question of Chinese immigration should be settled upon higher principles than those of a cold and selfish expediency," he argued in a speech in 1869. "There are such things in the world as human rights. They rest upon no conventional foundation, but are external, universal, and indestructible. Among these, is the right of locomotion; the right of migration; the right which belongs to no particular race, but belongs alike to all and to all alike. It is the right you assert by staying here, and your fathers asserted by coming here. It is this great right that I assert for the Chinese and Japanese, and for all other varieties of men equally with yourselves, now and forever."[5]

However, as immigrants poured into US cities in the late nineteenth and early twentieth centuries, black leaders changed their tune. Booker T. Washington worried that these newcomers would provide a supply of labor that gave employers yet another excuse not to hire black Americans. In his famous 1895 Atlanta Exposition speech, Washington said:

> To those of the white race who look to the incoming of those of foreign birth and strange tongue and habits for the prosperity of the South, were I permitted I would repeat what I say to my own race, "cast down your bucket where you are." Cast it down among the eight millions of Negroes whose habits you know, whose fidelity and love you have tested in days when to have proved treacherous meant the ruin of your firesides. Cast down your bucket among these people who have, without strikes and labour wars, tilled your fields, cleared your forests, built your railroads and cities, and brought forth treasures from the bowels of the earth, and helped make possible this magnificent representation of the progress of the South.[6]

Black newspapers and periodicals supported the Chinese Exclusion Act of 1882, and civil rights groups cheered legislation passed by Congress in the 1920s that targeted the influx of immigrants from southern and eastern Europe. A 1904 essay in *The Colored American Magazine* explaining "The Evils of European Emigration" noted that these new arrivals "readily afford a means by which commercial institutions may obtain cheap labor, thereby depriving native born Americans of the opportunity to work which is justly theirs." The "entrance of any considerable number of these emigrants into a community is generally a signal for reduction in wages," it continued. "It matters little to corporations whether or not native Americans are thrown out of employment. All they desire is cheap labor and whether or not such labor is furnished by Americans or foreigners is a matter which gives them little concern."[7]

The Trump White House, including influential advisers like Stephen Miller, likewise presented immigration as a zero-sum proposition. The assumption was that there is a fixed number of employment opportunities and that foreigners who came to the United States to work harmed the job prospects of those already here. It's an intuitive argument, but economists refer to it as the zero-sum *fallacy* for a reason. David Henderson of the Hoover Institution has used a nonimmigration example to illustrate.

Consider something that happened in the United States, especially since World War II, that, in its effect on the US labor force, resembles immigration: the entry of women into the labor force. Between 1950 and 2000, 47.2 million additional women and 31.4 million additional men entered the labor force. If jobs had been scarce, we should have seen the unemployment rate increase by many percentage points. It didn't. In fact, the unemployment rate for men, which was 4.8 percent in 1950, was down to 3.9 percent in 2000. The unemployment rate for women, which was 5.3 percent in 1950, was down to 4.1 percent in 2000. The same thing has happened with immigrants.[8]

The labor economist Richard Vedder and two co-authors juxtaposed immigration levels and the unemployment rates in the United States throughout most of the twentieth century. "Using several different periods and approaches, we consistently found no statistically meaningful relationship between immigration and unemployment," wrote Vedder. "However, if there is any correlation, it would appear to be negative: Higher immigration is associated with lower unemployment. For example, immigration reached its highest level (relative to the population) in the first 25 years of this [twentieth] century; the average annual U.S. unemployment rate was 5.05%; in the next 69 years of relatively smaller immigrant flows, the average unemployment rate was 7.38%."[9] In a 2018 paper that updated Vedder's research and added an analysis of how immigration levels impact labor force participation, the economist Madeline Zavodny found that a 1 percentage point increase in the share of the labor force comprised of immigrants appears to slightly "reduce the unemployment rate" and slightly "raise the labor force participation rate" of US natives in the same sex and education group. In short, "having more immigrants overall does not significantly affect U.S. natives' unemployment or labor force participation rate."[10]

What Vedder and Zavodny found nationally has proven to be the case at the state level as well. California has long been home to the nation's largest population of both legal and illegal immigrants. An Urban Institute study assessing the economic impact of significant migration to Southern California from Mexico concluded:

> To what extent did the influx of immigrants entering Southern California in the 1970s reduce the jobs available to nonimmigrant workers? The answer for the 1970s is little if at all. Although Hispanic workers filled a large proportion of the jobs added during the decade, particularly in manufacturing, there is no indication that work opportunities for nonimmigrants lessoned. Despite mass immigration to Southern California, unemployment rates rose less rapidly there than in the remainder of the nation. Furthermore, the labor-force participation rate (the proportion of the population in the labor force) did not seem to be affected. In fact the participation rate for both blacks and whites was higher in Southern California than elsewhere in the state and nation.[11]

Although black unemployment rates "are not increased—if anything, they are lowered—by a rise in the proportion of Mexican immigrants in a local labor market," the study did report that "wages in several occupations and industries rose more slowly in Los Angeles than elsewhere as low-skilled immigrants, primarily Hispanics, entered the labor force."[12] Other research has similarly concluded that low-skill immigration can negatively impact the wages of low-skill natives—namely US workers who lack a high-school diploma, a disproportionate number of whom are black. The question is the magnitude of this wage effect. Harvard labor economist George Borjas, for example, has estimated that US immigration between 1990 and 2010 resulted in a 3.1 percent wage reduction for high-school dropouts. For high school graduates and people with "some college," wages *rose* 0.4 percent and 0.9 percent, respectively. For college graduates and those with post-graduate degrees, immigration's effect on wages was an estimated –0.1 percent and –0.9 percent, respectively.[13] A 2014 paper by Giovanni Peri, an economist at the University of California, Davis, found even less of a negative wage impact for low-skill workers than Borjas did.[14] Again, the least-skilled workers were in fact hurt most, likely because they shared a similar skill set with the new arrivals. Still, immigration had a positive impact on the wages of other workers, and the overall effects in either direction were relatively small on balance. It's also worth noting that people without a high school degree represent a tiny segment of Americans, and that segment has been shrinking. In 2017, the drop-out rate was 4.7 percent among all groups and 5.5 percent among blacks.[15] The Bureau of Labor Statistics reports that only "6 percent of Blacks age 25 and older in the labor force had less than a high school diploma in 2018, down from 18 percent in 1992."[16] Nor should we assume that higher black unemployment rates are purely a function of not being able to find work. "For the most part, the foreign-born high school dropouts are Latino—many with limited English language ability and many who entered the United States illegally," writes economist Nicholas Eberstadt. "Despite 'living in the shadows,' they largely seem to have had no difficulty becoming part of the US labor force. One critical determinant to being in the US workforce today seems to be wanting to be there in the first place."[17]

Nevertheless, the Trump administration's anti-immigrant agenda was presented as a way to advantage US workers in general and black workers specifically. "We've seen significant reductions in wages for blue-collar workers, massive displacement of African American and Hispanic workers, as well as the displacement of immigrant workers from previous years who oftentimes compete directly against new arrivals who are being paid even less," White House adviser Stephen Miller said.[18] And here's Trump himself: "America proudly welcomes millions of lawful immigrants who enrich our society and contribute to our nation, but all Americans are hurt by uncontrolled illegal migration. It strains public resources

and drives down jobs and wages. Among those hardest hit
are African Americans and Hispanic Americans."[19] After
the pandemic struck in 2020, the administration argued that
even immigrants here legally posed a threat to black employment prospects. "Trump officials said that legal immigrants
'take away jobs,' and in the current virus-fed unemployment
crisis, they want to help Americans," wrote the *Washington
Examiner*. "The officials said that many of the jobs will be
attractive to low- to middle-income Americans eager to get
back to work, especially blacks, Hispanics, and lower-income
whites."[20]

THERE ARE OF COURSE many sensible reasons to reduce
illegal immigration as much as possible, and calling for better
border enforcement is not tantamount to racism, which was
the claim of many on the left during the Trump presidency.
We are a nation of laws, for starters, and illegal immigration
undermines the rule of law. We are also a sovereign country,
which ostensibly means that we get to choose who comes
here and under what circumstances. Our immigration regulations exist to benefit, first and foremost, the people who
live in the United States, not the people trying to get in. One
reason that Trump's attacks on illegal immigration resonated
with millions of voters—including many who typically voted
for Democrats—is that Americans don't like to see our laws

flouted. They don't like to see caravans of Central Americans arriving at the southern border and demanding entry, or trying to force their way in. And they don't like foreign migrants taking advantage of our generous asylum polices with bogus claims of persecution in their homelands. Polling has long shown Americans on balance to be quite immigrant-friendly. Democrats and Republicans alike display a great deal of sympathy for people who come here to work and in search of a better life, and majorities in both parties have supported allowing even those who came illegally to remain, provided they met certain requirements such as paying a fine and passing a criminal background check. Yet surveys also show that voters want the border fixed, rather than erased, and Trump promised to do that, albeit with limited success.

As we've seen, evidence that immigrants displace US workers of any race is not supported by most research at the state or national level. And while evidence does show a negative "wage effect" for Americans without a high school degree, the impact appears to be relatively small. One reason that immigration is more economically beneficial to the United States than the skeptics acknowledge is that we generally are not importing exact replicas of native workers. Immigrants, be they legal or illegal, tend to be either less-skilled and less-educated than the typical US native, or more skilled and more educated. They are more likely to compete for jobs with one another than with the native-born. There is some overlap, to be sure, such as with native high school dropouts. But, in the main, immigrants bring different abilities and a willingness to do different jobs, often at lower wages, which can result in lower prices. They are filling niches in our labor markets rather than nudging US workers out of jobs. We could persuade college graduates to pick lettuce in Arizona, but what are the trade-offs? How much would we have to pay them? What would that do to the price of groceries or dining out? And is that an efficient use of the country's human capital, or are we better off with more-educated individuals making more productive use of their abilities?

Equally important, immigrants aren't just workers. They are also consumers who purchase goods and services. They buy cars and get their nails done, thus increasing demand for those things. Companies respond to higher demand for their products by increasing output, which often requires hiring more people to expand operations. In this way immigrants also serve as job-multipliers. Any proper assessment of the economic impact of immigration must take into account the immigrant's role as both a worker and a consumer, yet the latter function is too often ignored.

Experience also teaches us that the US labor market isn't static, and that the number of jobs isn't finite. Between 2017 and 2019, the labor force grew from 160.3 million people to 163.5 million people,[21] while the national unemployment rate simultaneously *declined* in each of those years and ultimately reached a fifty-year low.[22] All of this happened without a new wall being built and without mass deportations of illegals. Indeed, it's by no means clear that the size of the unauthorized population in America fell at all under Trump. Mark Twain is said to have remarked that a man with a reputation as an early riser can sleep until noon. Did Trump coast on his reputation as an immigration hardliner?

The number of migrants apprehended at the border is used as a proxy for the level of illegal immigration in the United States. When apprehensions are up, it means that illegal entries are rising. According to the US Customs and Border Protection agency, apprehensions fell by 115,000 in 2017, Trump's first year in office. But they rose dramatically over the next two years—more than doubling from 404,000 to 859,000 between 2018 and 2019—before declining sharply in the wake of Covid.[23] The issue here is not why illegal immigration, as measured by border apprehensions, rose under Trump. I'm simply noting that it did in fact rise and that such data undermine not only claims to the contrary but also notions that restrictive immigration policies redounded to the benefit black workers in general.

According to the Migration Policy Institute, the size of the illegal population in the United States prior to the pandemic had changed only modestly over the past decade.[24] The makeup of that population shifted, but the overall number of people in the country illegally was relatively flat. "While the number of unauthorized immigrants in the United States has been largely stable over the past decade, there have been notable changes in the composition of the population, which has seen a sizeable drop in Mexicans alongside increased arrivals from other world regions, especially Asia and Central America," reads a press release for the report. "The number of unauthorized immigrants from Mexico fell from 7.6 million in 2007, right before the onset of the Great Recession, to 5.5 million in 2018, a new Migration Policy Institute (MPI) fact sheet finds. During the same period, the unauthorized population from Asia rose from 866,000 to 1.5 million, and the Central American one from 1.5 million to 1.8 million."[25] Overall, the report shows, the illegal immigration population *grew* from 10.5 million in 2017 to 11 million the following year.

Keep in mind that MPI is a think tank that advocates for more immigration. But organizations that call for fewer immigrants, such as the Center for Immigration Studies (CIS), reached a similar conclusion. Trump did not reduce the legal or illegal immigration populations in absolute terms so much as retard their growth. As Steven A. Camarota, CIS's director of research, wrote a week before Trump was voted out of office, "Census Bureau data from the 2019 American Community Survey (ACS) show that in the first two years of the Trump administration, growth in the immigrant population (legal and illegal) averaged only about 200,000 a year, which stands in stark contrast with the roughly 650,000 a year from 2010 to 2017."[26]

Reducing the severity of a negative trend like illicit border crossings is not nothing, but the question here is what practical impact it had on the employment prospects of blacks.

Historically, black job opportunities have not been conditioned on lower levels of immigration. Between 1900 and 1930, for example, the immigration population grew from 10.3 to 14.2 million, an increase of nearly 38 percent.[27] Yet over this same period, and notwithstanding the concerns of some black leaders mentioned earlier, black employment rates *exceeded* those of whites.[28] More recently, a 2012 study of census data by University of Denver economist Jack Strauss found that metropolitan areas with higher levels of immigration from Latin America had lower poverty rates, lower unemployment rates, and higher wages among blacks. According to Strauss:

> For every 1% increase in a city's share of Latinos, African American median and mean wages increase by 3%. This relationship is large. Consider St. Louis, which has 1.5% of its population from Latin America. If St. Louis were to have a Latino population share as large as other large metropolitan areas, African American wages would be approximately 30% higher.[29]

Stuart Anderson is the executive director of the National Foundation for American Policy, a nonpartisan research group, and a former high-ranking official in the Immigration and Naturalization Service during the George W. Bush administration. Citing Department of Homeland Security figures, Anderson told me that deportations did in fact increase prior to the pandemic under Trump, from roughly

287,000 in 2017 to 360,000 in 2019. But the average was still below what took place under his predecessor. For the first six years of the Obama presidency, for example, annual deportations never fell below 379,000, and from 2010 to 2014, they averaged more than 400,000 per year.[30]

"Some people overestimate the effectiveness Trump had in addressing illegal immigration and whether it would have helped black workers even if Trump's policies had been effective," said Anderson. "While making more work visas available would dramatically reduce illegal entry, Trump's enforcement-only approach had a minimal impact on limiting illegal immigration, and, in any case, there is little evidence that people here illegally have much, if any, impact on the economic prospects of black workers."[31]

Again, the focus here is not on *why* Trump didn't deport more illegal immigrants than Obama. The question is whether the official data back his supporters' claims that he did, and whether reductions in immigrant labor play an important role in black economic advancement. Alex Nowrasteh, who follows immigration policy for the libertarian Cato Institute, told me that he believes Trump would have done more to reduce illegal immigration but met resistance not only from Congress but at the state and local level, too. He also said it's important to keep the size of today's illegal population in perspective when assessing its impact on black workers. "There were approximately 44 million black Americans and 10.5 million illegal immigrants during the first year of the Trump administration," said Nowrasteh. "If Trump decreases the number of illegal immigrants by a few hundred thousand . . . that decline couldn't possibly have much of an effect on the wages of millions of black Americans, to say nothing of millions of other Americans."[32]

The reality is that however many millions of immigrants, legal or illegal, resided in the United States during the Trump administration, black unemployment rates reached record lows, black poverty rates reached record lows, and black wages rose at a faster rate than their white counterparts. Nationally, the number of available jobs was significantly larger than the number of people looking for work. At one point in 2019, for example, there were 7.4 million job openings and only 5.8 million job seekers. Whether you believe there are 10 million, 15 million, or 20 million illegal immigrants in the country, the United States was still experiencing a significant *labor shortage*. The *Wall Street Journal* reported at the time that "the number of job openings exceeded the number of unemployed Americans by the largest margin on record in April, signaling difficulty for employers to find workers in a historically tight market."[33] Notwithstanding our leaky borders, America experienced a worker *deficit* in the run-up to the pandemic even while Trump and his supporters insisted that illegal immigrants were "stealing" jobs. That is not an argument for ignoring illegal immigration, but it does suggest that the Trump administration's concerns about foreign workers displacing Americans and depressing wages were largely off base.

CHAPTER 3

The Minimum Wage Canard

≥≤

THE INVESTMENT BANK Goldman Sachs released a paper in March 2019 that showed pay for those at the lower end of the wage distribution, where blacks are concentrated, rising at nearly double the rate of pay for those at the upper end. Average hourly earnings were growing at rates that hadn't been seen in almost a decade, but what "has set this rise apart is that it's the first time during the economic recovery that began in mid-2009 that the bottom half of earners are benefitting more that the top half—in fact, about twice as much" reported CNBC.

Citing a graph included in Goldman's analysis, CNBC added that the "trend began in 2018"—the first year that the economy felt the full impact of Donald Trump's corporate tax cuts—"and has continued into this year and could be signaling a stronger economy than many experts think."[1] The Goldman findings were largely ignored by most other media outlets, where any narrowing of income inequality, when acknowledged at all during the Trump years, was usually credited to the previous administration. In addition, Trump's political adversaries and their friends in the press made a habit of attributing higher pay among low-income workers to minimum wage hikes at the state and local level. "In his State of the Union address Tuesday, President Trump touted a 'blue collar boom,' noting that wages are rising fastest for low-income workers," USA Today reported in February 2020. "He's correct, but Trump left out one thing: a large portion of those gains can be traced to minimum wage increases in more than half the states."[2] The New York Times had hit a similar theme a few weeks earlier in an article headlined, "Pay Is Rising Fastest for Low Earners. One Reason? Minimum Wages."[3]

Nor were reporters the only ones suggesting that lifting the wage floor by mandate played a larger role than tighter labor markets in rising pay for low earners. "One reason that workers at the bottom are doing relatively better recently is the recent increases in many state and local minimum wages," wrote economists Ryan Nunn and Jay Shambaugh in a 2020 paper for the Brookings Institution. "While the federal minimum wage has not risen since 2009, many states—such as California and Massachusetts—and cities, such as Seattle and New York City, have increased their legislated minimums considerably."[4] Two economists at the University of California, Berkeley, Ellora Derenoncourt and Claire Montialoux, have argued that the "earnings difference between white and black workers fell dramatically in the

United States in the late 1960s and early 1970s" and that "the expansion of the minimum wage played a critical role in this decline."[5] If Donald Trump exaggerated the negative effects of immigration on black workers, was there was a corollary in how his political opponents exaggerated the positive effects of minimum wage hikes?

Since 1995, the federal minimum wage has increased five times—in 1996, 1997, 2007, 2008, and 2009—from $4.25 to $7.25. In 1995, nine states had minimum wages above the federal level. By 2020, the number had grown to 29 states, plus Washington, DC. One problem with citing minimum wage increases as a significant driver of pay hikes in the United States is the dearth of workers who earn the minimum. In 2017, for example, there were 80.4 million workers paid at hourly rates, and just 2.3 percent of them were paid at or below the federal minimum wage.[6] The percentage of workers who earn at or below the state minimum wage, which can be higher than the federal minimum, is also quite small. In 2015, it was just under 8 percent.[7] In addition to this quantitative problem, a state minimum wage increase is typically a one-off. If it takes effect on January 1 of a particular year, for example, you expect to see wage growth in January. You would not expect see wages continue to rise in February, March, April, May, and so on, yet that is what happened to wages in the years prior to the pandemic under Trump.

In 2006, the economists David Neumark and William L. Wascher published a review of more than 100 studies on how the minimum wage affects employment. They concluded that "among the papers we view as providing the most credible evidence, almost all point to negative employment effects, both for the United States as well as for many other countries." The authors added: "Two other important conclusions emerge from our review. First, we see very few—if any—studies that provide convincing evidence of positive employment effects of minimum wages." Second, "the studies that focus on the least-skilled groups provide relatively overwhelming evidence of stronger disemployment effects for these groups."[8] In a follow-up study released in 2021, Neumark and co-author Peter Shirley looked at academic papers published since 1992. They found that nearly 80 percent of the studies showed negative employment effects from minimum wage increases in the form of fewer jobs or hours; that the negative impact is strongest for teenagers, young adults, and people with less education; and that there was no indication that these negative effects had eased in the studies from more recent years.[9] Although the *New York Times's* Paul Krugman and other liberals claimed that, based on a handful of newer studies, there's "just no evidence that raising the minimum wage costs jobs," those studies remain outliers, just as they always have been.[10]

When I asked Neumark about the impact of recent state minimum wage increases, he said that "inequality falls when you raise the minimum wage. That has to happen. But there's ample evidence that there are some hours reductions and employment reductions, so there are some offsets there. That's one reason why they [minimum wage increases] haven't played a big role" in reducing economic inequality. "I certainly don't think they had anything to do with declining unemployment" under Trump, he said. "If anything, they probably eliminated job opportunities. There are lower-wage groups, so the [higher] minimum will push their wages up more than others, but that's all conditional on having a job. No one thinks the minimum wage is more important than the business cycle. A booming labor market will swamp any minimum wage increase we would do."[11]

While calling for a $15 federal minimum wage in 2021, Rep. Nancy Pelosi said that "27 million people would get a raise, 70% of them women."[12] Realistically, Pelosi had no idea how many people would get a raise because she didn't know how many people would keep their jobs. Nor did she know how many people who kept their jobs would see reduced hours due to the new higher minimum. Finally, she didn't know how many people would never be hired in the first place because the mandated higher wage floor had priced them out of the labor market. These are the trade-offs that are so often ignored by minimum wage proponents. Around the time of Pelosi's remark, the Congressional Budget Office reported that an estimated 1.4 million jobs would vanish if the federal minimum wage was increased to $15 per hour.[13] Other research challenges the congresswoman's reference to how women would be affected.

Liberals regularly insist that minimum wage increases are an effective means of addressing poverty, and they like to hold up single working moms as typical minimum wage earners. However, a 2014 study found that the vast majority of workers who would benefit from a minimum wage hike live in households that are above the poverty line. According to one of the study's authors, economist Joseph Sabia, "only 13 percent of workers who would be affected live in poor households, while nearly two-thirds live in households with incomes over twice the poverty line, and over 40 percent live in households with incomes over three times the poverty line."[14] Most minimum wage recipients are not impoverished or the family's sole breadwinner. Many are teenagers living at home, or seniors working part time to stay busy in retirement. Not only are most minimum wage earners not poor, but most poor people already make more than the minimum wage. What poor households need most is a job, not a minimum wage hike, and to the extent that raising the minimum reduces employment opportunities, it can exacerbate both racial and economic inequality.

In 2015, Seattle became the first major city to pass legislation that would increase the minimum wage incrementally to $15 an hour over a multiyear period. The following year, the University of Washington published a report on how the ordinance impacted low-income earners. "Seattle's low-wage workers did see larger-than-usual paychecks . . . in late 2015, but most—if not all—of that increase was due to a strong local economy," the study concluded. "Increased wages were off-set by modest reductions in employment and hours, thereby limiting the extent to which higher wages directly translated into higher average earnings." Another study published by the National Bureau of Economic Research the next year found a similar result, concluding that Seattle's minimum wage increase "reduced hours worked in low-wage jobs by about 9 percent, while hourly wages in such jobs increased by around 3 percent. Consequently, total payroll fell for such jobs, implying that the minimum wage ordinance lowered low-wage employees' earnings by an average of $125 per month in 2016."[15]

Because low-income minorities are overrepresented among less-skilled and less-experienced workers, they stand to lose the most when labor costs go up. When the economists William Even and David Macpherson looked at the impact of state minimum wage hikes from 2007 to 2009, they found that the increases cost younger blacks more jobs than the Great Recession did. Among white males ages sixteen to twenty-four, each 10 percent increase in a federal or state minimum wage decreased employment by 2.5 percent. For Hispanic males, the figure was 1.2 percent. "But among black males in this group, each 10% increase in the minimum wage decreased employment by 6.5%."[16]

For anyone familiar with the origins of minimum wage laws in the United States, such findings are not surprising. Historically, it has been the proponents of wage mandates, including unions and their political backers, who have exhibited animus toward blacks. For early proponents, racial disparities in outcome weren't merely a byproduct of these laws. It was the intent. Unions support minimum wage laws out of self-interest, not because they benefit workers per se. Union members already make more than the minimum, but they understand that having a minimum wage mandate in place insulates them from having to compete for jobs with nonunion members, who may be willing to work for less money. At the urging of labor unions, which at the time excluded black members, Congress passed several laws in the 1930s that were aimed at preventing blacks from competing with whites by working at lower wages. These measures included the Davis-Bacon Act of 1931, the National Industrial Recovery Act of 1933, the National Labor Relations Act of 1935, and the Fair Labor Standards Act of 1938, which established the first federal minimum wage. The laws are cited by many on the left as "pro-worker," though it would be more accurate to say that black workers progressed economically notwithstanding these laws rather than because of them. In 1930, the black employment rate was slightly lower than the white employment rate, but that soon changed.

"The National Labor Relations Act of 1935, which promoted unionization, also tended to price black workers out of jobs, in addition to union rules that kept blacks from jobs by barring them from union membership," wrote the economist Thomas Sowell. "The National Recovery Act raised wage rates in the Southern textile industry by 70 percent in just five months, and its impact nationwide was estimated to have cost blacks half a million jobs."[17] Lawmakers at the time did not hide their racial motives. During hearings on Davis-Bacon, which regulates wages on federal construction projects, Rep. William Upshaw of Georgia spoke of "the real problem" of a "superabundance or large aggregation of Negro labor." Rep. John Cochran of Missouri, who also backed the bill, spoke of "numerous complaints in recent months" about "low-paid colored mechanics" pushing whites out of jobs. Rep. Miles Clayton Allgood of Alabama told a story about a contractor from his state who travelled to New York with "cheap colored labor that he transports, and he puts them in cabins, and it is labor of that sort that is in competition with white labor throughout the country." William Green, the head of the American Federation of Labor, complained that "colored labor is being sought to demoralize wage rates."[18] In the ensuing decades, Congress would continue to raise the minimum wage, and competition from black workers would continue to be invoked by proponents as a justification. When he was a US senator from Massachusetts in the 1950s, John F. Kennedy backed increases to the minimum wage as a way of protecting New England industry from Southern competition. "Having on the market a rather large source of cheap labor depresses wages outside that group, too—the wages of the white worker who has to compete," he told an NAACP official testifying at a hearing in 1957. "And when an employer can substitute a colored worker at a lower wage—and there are, as you pointed out, these hundreds of thousands looking for decent work—it affects the whole wage structure of an area, doesn't it?"[19] Whether or not the intent today is to dampen black job prospects by raising the minimum wage, that is the reality.

In 1966, as part of Lyndon Johnson's Great Society push, Congress amended the Fair Labor Standards Act to extend its minimum wage provisions to more workers. Ellora Derenoncourt and Claire Montialoux, two economists at the University of California, Berkeley, have argued that Congress's decision "to both raise the minimum wage and expand it to workers in previously unprotected industries led to a significant drop in earnings inequality between Black and white Americans."[20] But what was happening to black earnings prior to 1966? As noted earlier, in the 1940s and 1950s, incomes of black men and women were already growing at a significantly faster pace than their white counterparts', which is to say that economic inequality was already shrinking as blacks migrated to cities, increased their years of education, and took advantage of tighter labor markets associated with World War II.[21] "By the mid-1940s, the national per capita income of African Americans stood at $779, compared to $1,140 for whites," according to the historian Robert Weems. However, "in some locales," including Washington, DC, and Cleveland, "urban blacks possessed a per capita income higher than the national white average."[22] As also noted earlier, between 1940 and 1960, which is prior to the minimum wage expansions that Derenoncourt and Montialoux credit with reducing income inequality, black poverty rates fell by 40 percentage points, which is faster than the rate at which white poverty declined. The authors want to credit minimum wage expansions with improvements in black economic outcomes, but the improvements predate the expansions. "The huge decline in black poverty between 1940 and 1960 occurred well before the Civil Rights Act of 1964 outlawed Jim Crow practices in employment, education and public accommodations," wrote Stephan Thernstrom and Abigail Thernstrom in *America in Black and White*. "It also was well before the advent of the War on Poverty and various other Great Society programs designed to uplift the poor."[23] It's true that, following the expansion of minimum wage mandates in the 1960s, black incomes continued to rise and black poverty continued to fall, at least for a short time, but both trends decelerated in pace. Between 1960 and 1970, black poverty fell by 13 percentage points. During the decade of the 1970s, it fell by just 1 percentage point.[24] Meanwhile, black incomes lost ground to white incomes. In 1970, the black median household income was 60.9 percent of white median household income. By 1980, the black median had fallen to 57.6 percent of the white median.[25]

≶

WHAT IMMIGRATION RESTRICTIONISM and minimum wage laws have in common is that both make labor markets less flexible than they would be otherwise. Historically, blacks have experienced far more dramatic economic gains when there is less such government interference, when labor markets are tight, and when the economy is expanding beyond the 2 percent Obama-era norm. Donald Trump's policies were far from hands-off, but by comparison to those of his immediate predecessor, the country experienced an economy that was more conducive to rapid economic growth, and blacks were able to share in the resulting prosperity in ways that they previously had not.

The Covid-19 pandemic ended this short Trump boom prematurely. Tens of millions of jobs were wiped out in 2020 as the economy screeched to a halt to address the devastating virus. We'll never know if the preceding prosperity would have continued apace, of course. We'll never know how Trump's trade wars would have affected growth in China and Europe in the long run and thus ultimately have affected growth in the United States. We'll never know how his continued efforts to reduce the absolute number of foreign workers in the country would have impacted certain industries' ability to hire employees at wages that allowed businesses to stay competitive, or even to stay open.

What we do know is that the economic gains we saw in the first three years of the Trump administration were real, were significant, and were more than merely a continuation of what was happening under Barack Obama. We know that blacks and other low-income minorities benefited disproportionately from Trump's economic policies. And we know that Trump did not get the credit he deserved for the economy's robust performance on his watch because most of the intelligentsia, including an overtly hostile mainstream media, consciously played down or ignored his successes. Nevertheless, what was happening in the pre-pandemic economy deserves our attention, not for partisan reasons but because it offers more evidence of what kinds of public policies have tended to deliver sustained economic growth along with reductions in racial inequality—and what kinds have tended to do neither.

PART 2

≽≼

Dissenting Points of View

CHAPTER 4
Boom or Echo?

—— ❧ ——

JUAN WILLIAMS

EARLIER IN THESE PAGES, Jason Riley makes an eye-opening claim.

The Trump economy, he writes, "benefitted low-income minorities more than anyone."

And here is another surprise—this one with a political punch.

Riley writes that many black and Hispanic voters "found themselves better off under Donald Trump than under his predecessor."

That means President Trump did more for blacks and other minorities than the nation's first black president, Barack Obama. Keep in mind that polls show Trump is regarded as a racist by most black Americans (83 percent in a January 2020 Washington Post-IPSOS poll) as well as by Americans of all colors (52 percent in a June 2020 Yahoo News /You.gov poll).[1]

The central pillar to Riley's arguments is the indisputable fact that black and Hispanic unemployment and poverty rates sank to record lows during the Trump presidency.

Also, to bolster his point, Riley correctly notes that black and Hispanic workforce participation increased under Trump.

That is all good news.

Riley attributes the progress on minority economic standing to Trump pursuing policies of "lower taxes and lighter regulation."

And he upbraids Trump's critics, specifically left-leaning journalists, for ignoring the good news.

These reporters and columnists closed their eyes to Trump's success in improving the job picture for blacks and Latinos, Riley argues, because the story did not fit their view that Trump is hostile to racial minorities.

Unlike the other Trump critics cited by Riley, I am open to this good news.

If Trump created a new formula for black economic advancement, then he deserves praise. And his formula deserves to be replicated as a model for further improvement.

Riley and I are both black men. We want to move forward on long-standing racial economic imbalances in the United States, the world's top economy.

But I think there is a problem with Riley's evidence.

If Trump's tax cuts and scaling back business regulation greatly improved economic outcomes for minority groups, how is it that most of the improvement took place under President Obama?

Obama's economic policies might be described as the exact opposite of Trump's policies.

Obama raised taxes and put in place more business regulation. He also got Congress to approve a larger social safety net, notably the controversial Affordable Care Act.

Yet, during Obama's tenure black unemployment fell more sharply than it did during Trump's time in office. And it fell at a faster rate.

Black unemployment declined from 16.8 percent in March of 2010 to 7.8 percent in January of 2017—with economic policy under Obama's control.

Trump later reduced black unemployment to 5.4 percent by August of 2019.

Those numbers, hard facts, indicate that declines in black unemployment can't be attributed to introduction of any new economic policies introduced after Trump entered the White House.

The more widely accepted explanation of the improvement in the economic picture for black Americans while Trump was president is that it is tied to momentum from years of slow and steady economic gains under President Obama's earlier policies.

Obama is credited with spurring an economic recovery from the 2009 recession through the end of his term in January 2017. That period of rising GDP (gross domestic product) set a record for the third-longest period of economic growth in U.S. history.

That is the context in which most of the improvement in black employment took place. It began under Obama's presidency and later continued during the recovery started under his guidance.

In addition to the lion's share of black economic progress taking place under Obama, black unemployment dropped at a faster rate under Obama than it did under Trump.

A comparison of economic data during the last three years of the two presidencies, by Joe Davidson of the *Washington Post*, found much faster gains in economic well-being for blacks and other minorities while Obama was president.[2]

In Obama's last three years, from December 2013 to December 2016 there was a 4 percent decrease in black unemployment, from 11.9 percent to 7.9 percent, a drop of about a third.

In Trump's last three years, from February 2017 to February 2020, there was a 2.1 percent decrease in black unemployment, from 7.9 percent to 5.8 percent, a decline of "just over one-fourth," wrote Davidson.[3]

It is fair to credit Trump with not interrupting the downward trajectory of black unemployment began under Obama.

But it is not fair to say that Trump deserves credit for a record low black unemployment rate without mentioning that it is part of the larger story of progress that began before he took office.

And, again, it is important to note that so much progress took place under Obama, a president who raised taxes on the rich and increased government regulation, notably on banks and Wall Street investors.

It is also worth noting that under Trump, changes in black unemployment took place in sync with spikes and declines in rates of employment for other racial groups: whites, Asian Americans, and Hispanic Americans.

"In general, these unemployment rates tend to move together," Danielle Kurtzleben wrote in an NPR fact check in January of 2018. The black and Hispanic employment picture did not change "in any remarkable way, relative to other groups' unemployment rates."[4]

There are other measures of black economic progress that add to the case that Obama deserves the lion's share of credit for improving the economic outlook for black Americans.

For example, look at the broad metric of median household income for black and white Americans.

The Associated Press reported that median household income was higher for blacks in 2000, years before Trump took office, than at any time under Trump's time in the White House.[5]

In addition, the income inequality between blacks and whites grew during Trump's tenure. Specifically, the gap between blacks and whites in wealth—stocks, bonds, real estate, savings—worsened with Trump in the White House.

Riley cites a study that found "higher income groups saw weekly wages grow by larger dollar amounts" than among low-income groups. He interprets that as good news for the working class and poor because low-income groups saw a higher percentage rise in their wages than high-income groups.

Here is different perspective on the faster growth of black family wealth as compared to white family wealth under Trump. It comes from a September 2020 report done by the program MarketWatch: "The faster pace of growth for blacks is off a smaller baseline figure, and as a result the span between whites and blacks actually widened slightly."[6]

The bottom line here is that income equality got worse under Trump. And most black people were on the wrong end of that outcome.

And the same logic holds for comparing unemployment rates across racial lines.

"Even as the overall unemployment rate dropped after a sharp rise in March [of 2020 when fear of the spread of Corona Virus dragged down the American economy], the black unemployment rate remained higher," wrote Fabiola Cineas on the website Vox. "White Americans found work more quickly overall and the [racial] unemployment gap persisted."[7]

My point in citing the Vox article is that even with the higher levels of black employment, the black unemployment rate never was as low as the white unemployment rate, under Obama or Trump.

I still give Riley major credit for thinking outside the box.

His line of economic argument is hopeful. He is looking for better ideas to deal with consistently high rates of minority unemployment.

For example, he specifically points to the economic boost that comes with maintaining two-parent families. I agree wholeheartedly. And black Americans sadly lag in this category.

Similarly, he notes higher levels of education contribute to higher levels of employment. Once again, I agree with Riley. There is no argument with that correlation.

He also points to the benefit of people moving to areas with lots of jobs, specifically the period of history when large numbers of black people moved out of the rural, impoverished areas of the South and into the industrialized North.

He points to labor force participation as another key predictor of black economic success. Again, I agree with him.

It is essential for everyone, but especially for young black Americans, to move out of economically depressed areas. Finding their way to suburbs and cities flush with jobs is a step anyone can take to help themselves by improving their chances of getting a job.

That one step also opens the door to other economic opportunities, beginning with improving their résumés and building a network of people who, as they rise in the economy, may be able to hire their colleagues.

Yes, these ideas about how to improve black and Latino economic outcomes are strong.

But these ideas existed before Trump's presidency.

They are not tied to Trump's economic policies.

I also applaud Riley for encouraging a level playing field.

The free market economic policies he advocates are strong because they avoid divisive, tribal fights over whether one racial group is helped and another is hurt due to government sponsored, race-based policies.

Riley is proposing a free market with no affirmative action involved, no use of racial set-asides for government contracts, and no hint of any reparations for past racial bias in these policies. Nowhere does a truly free market allow for the use of racial preference offered to achieve statistical equality based on race.

The brilliance of this idea is that it might be a way to escape America's swamp of racial politics. The rise in racial diversity in the United States in the last fifty years has been accompanied by less public and corporate acceptance of racism.

The idea of avoiding policies that focus on racial differences is very attractive right now.

All Americans, regardless of race, can see themselves moving up in that economy.

The downside of that idea is that despite progress, racial bias—in education, hiring, housing, health outcomes, and beyond—remains a fact of life.

Ignoring that reality is to excuse a status quo of black economic disadvantage.

Riley is an optimist, though.

He is committed to the idea that the best prescription for black economic gain is to focus on improving the economy for everyone instead of getting stuck in fights over racial inequality.

The aphorism tied to this idea is well-known: "A rising tide lifts all boats." The saying is often attributed to President Kennedy as he made the case for tax cuts in the 1960s. President Reagan also used it as he advanced tax cuts in the 1980s.

The counterpoint was best expressed by Jesse Jackson in his 1984 speech to the Democratic National Convention.

"Rising tides don't lift all boats, particularly those [people] stuck at the bottom," said Jackson, the civil rights activist who ran for the Democratic 1988 presidential nomination.

Jackson identified boats "at the bottom" as people who can be seen in the so-called Misery Index. That metric includes Americans caught in the grip of high levels of poverty, people in need of food stamps, people with children relying on free school lunch programs. Then there are people on Social Security, Medicare, Medicaid, and disability benefits who also qualify for the Misery Index.[8]

Even if the stock market and the overall economy improves, and lifts the upper half of American earners to higher levels of income, those at the bottom of the economy find themselves deeper under water.

And when taxes are cut and government social safety net programs are reduced as a result, the people in the Misery Index are vulnerable to economic distresses.

The dichotomy between Kennedy's "rising tide" and Jackson's boats "at the bottom" illuminates two strains of thought on economic inequality.

Riley is clearly in the Reagan/Kennedy camp. It is a camp that has been championed by Milton Friedman, Thomas Sowell, and other conservative economic thinkers.

But this belief in the power of unbridled capitalism, freed from the restraint of government regulation and taxation, is also a get-out-of-jail card for anyone anxious to be free of responsibility for the economic gains made by whites when racial barriers put blacks pursuing economic opportunity at a clear disadvantage.

That includes periods of legal slavery, government enforced racial segregation, and private sector acceptance of racial bias as a cultural standard for doing business.

Racial discrimination did not stop the U.S. economy from rising to become the most powerful in the world. As it gained strength the U.S. economy still limited the jobs available to the Irish, Italians and Jews, as well as to blacks and Hispanics and Asians—any group of Americans viewed as distinct from the white Protestant mainstream.

The impact on blacks was particularly harsh, keeping them out of even entry-level positions.

The same was true for educational opportunities, union cards, and apprentice training programs.

This discrimination against blacks limited free-market competition. Only white Protestants had the chance to get into the best schools and hold the best jobs.

It might as well be called affirmative action for White Anglo-Saxon Protestants.

Even with the legal segregation still governing the economy, Riley contends that black people made more economic advancement than they did after civil rights protests led the government to begin dismantling racial barriers.

Citing academic studies, Riley writes that "most scholars agree that income levels by race converged at the greatest rate between 1940 and 1970."

Similarly, he quotes scholars who write that the gap between black and white students graduating from high school "improved dramatically between the 1940s and the early 1970s," and subsequent improvements in the pace of black high school graduation slowed with black students never reaching the same graduation level as whites.

"This sort of empirical evidence is regularly ignored by those who cite the enduring effects of slavery, Jim Crow, redlining, public school segregation and employer discrimination to explain today's racial disparities in everything from labor force participation and income to educational attainment and criminal behavior," Riley writes.

Riley caps his argument by saluting black people "who lived during the ugliest decades of Jim Crow and much closer to the institution of slavery [yet] were able to outperform blacks in later generations who lived under black police chiefs, mayors, governors, senators and a twice-elected black president."

There is no argument that black people who made progress in the late nineteenth century and early twentieth century had a tough climb.

It is also true that the first half of the twentieth century saw erosion of strict racial discrimination in employment with the advent of two world wars, followed by wars in Korea and Vietnam. During that time the military and major military industries were desegregated.

The economic boom after World War II was especially important. From the 1930s through the 1960s, there was increased government social spending from the New Deal and later the Great Society.

The same period of the 1940s–1970s saw American professional sports allow nonwhites to play for the first time.

In addition, during that period the Supreme Court ruled against racial segregation in public schools, transit, and more.

As a result, today America has its largest black middle class in history. The changing landscape of economic opportunity for black people is obvious. So, too, are remaining points of racial difference, outright racial bias, and economic inequities.

Taking all of that into consideration, the nation is making progress on race.

But even if some of that progress on the economic front took place while Trump was in office, it is hard to ignore the momentum set in place by the prior administration's very different economic policies. And it is hard to ignore the decades of historic change that contributed to racial progress continuing in some other areas despite Trump being in office.

CHAPTER 5

The Wages of Immigration

—— ≥≤ ——

WILFRED REILLY

IN *THE BLACK BOOM*, Jason Riley correctly notes that the national media almost invariably attributed Donald Trump's success to racism, but that empirical data dispute this narrative. Instead, he argues that the success of policies such as 2017's Tax Cut and Jobs Act improved day-to-day life for working-class voters, and that this was reflected in opinion polling and at the ballot box.

Two of Riley's claims, however, strike me as wanting for evidence. One is that illegal immigration has few negative effects on lower-income voters, and the other is that Trump was too harsh on this issue. But Riley does an excellent job of illustrating the disconnect between the "woke" perspective common among the media elite and the more practical perspective shared by the majority of everyday Americans.

As Riley points out, Trump won a smaller percentage of whites, and "more blacks, Hispanics, and Asians," than Mitt Romney in 2012. In 2016, Trump was elected largely because of support from white working-class voters who had previously backed Barack Obama. This performance among people of color and working-class voters improved in 2020, when Trump lost to former Obama vice president Joe Biden but won 12 percent of the black vote, 32 percent of the Latino vote, and 47 percent of the Cuban American vote.

Riley posits an extremely plausible explanation for all of this: voters *liked* many of Trump's policies. Trump was, if nothing else, a businessman, and his administration focused on lowering taxes and lightening regulatory burdens in order to spur economic growth. In pursuit of this goal, he championed the Tax Cut and Jobs Act of 2017, which included a restructuring of corporate tax rates designed to boost investment by U.S. businesses on the home front.

Trump also targeted "major" regulations, generally defined as bureaucratic mandates or restrictions that impose a cost of $100,000,000 or more on business or industry. Amazingly, the Obama administration imposed roughly 600 new regulations at this level inside of eight years—including a set of HVAC efficiency standards that cost manufacturers $12.3 billion and reduced employment in that field by almost one third. Per Riley, Trump did away with several regulations of this sort and cut the rate of new rule making by more than 30 percent.

While there are arguments against economic policies of this kind, a substantial body of hard data indicates that Trump's moves did in fact stimulate the U.S. economy, often in ways that primarily benefitted people of color and the poor. Between 2017 and 2019, household income grew by 15.4 percent among blacks versus 11.5 percent among whites. During the first 11 full quarters of the Trump Presidency, wages for the bottom 10 percent of gainfully employed earners rose by 5.9 percent on an annual basis. By another metric, weekly wages for the poor grew by an average of $4.24 per quarter under Trump versus 88 cents per quarter under President Obama. Riley points out that, while black unemployment under Barack Obama reached its highest level in 25 years, black (and working-class) economic performance under Trump hit highs "not seen for generations."

Trump's economic success was not due simply—or primarily—to his inheriting a positively trending economy from Barack Obama. Riley is correct that, in 2016, the consensus view across the Treasury Department and the Fed was that the economy had reached full employment and would not grow faster under then-current policies. Although this has been almost forgotten, former Obama economic official Larry Summers predicted a 60 percent chance of a major recession before 2018. The forty-fourth president certainly did some good things for the economy, but there is no doubt that the *actual* 2016–2019 trend lines for major economic indicators, such as wages for low-skill workers, were well above anything projected before Donald Trump took office.

Riley is not correct about every Trump policy, or the relationship between the perceived impact of that policy and working-class voter attitudes. The author of the pro-immigration book *Let Them In*, Riley has always struck me as having a sizable soft spot for mass immigration and even illegal immigration, and this is again on display in *The Black Boom*. On multiple occasions, he seems to describe Trump's immigration policies as too strict, and he claims that mass immigration has little negative impact on minority and low-wage workers.

On one occasion he argues that immigrants are not "exact replicas of native workers," but instead folks who bring new and needed skills to the United States, and compete more with one another than with the native-born. At another point, he contends that post-1965 mass migration and the post–World War II movement of women into the labor force did not boost unemployment significantly, if at all. Beyond that, immigrants, both legal and illegal, "are . . . consumers" as well as workers, who purchase services and goods, and so enrich their new country: "They buy cars, and get their nails done." And so on.

Riley is more of a pure libertarian on this issue than I am. Unemployment (varying between 5.3 percent and 4.1 percent) may indeed have been stable between 1950 and 2000, but wages have also been stable in constant dollars since 1973,[1] with a decades-long trend of upward growth ending at almost the same time when those new pairs of hands came flooding into U.S. factories. Wage reduction, instead of unemployment, seems to be the primary negative effect of large-scale migration. Immigrants are solid people who come to the

United States to work, but they often do so at low wages, driving down pay for Americans and "creating" low-paying secondary jobs focused on providing services needed by working-class communities. One major study cited by Riley himself hardly debunks this point: Harvard economist George Borjas points out that immigration into the United States between 1990 and 2010 caused a 3.1 percent reduction in wages for poorly educated men.

It must also be noted that 2021 America is hardly the America of the Wild West era, full of bold *gaucho*-style laborers striving to make their way in a new land. Today, the United States is one of the world's largest welfare states, and immigrants in many demographic groups (e.g., young mothers) often choose not to work at all. A stunning 2018 report from the Center for Immigration Studies found that 63 percent of immigrant households take advantage of at least one major U.S. welfare program versus 35 percent of citizen households.[2] Any working-class black or white house-holder successful enough to pay taxes might logically view this as behavior one should oppose, and it is not clear that these voters did (or should have) penalized Trump for his hardline stance on immigration.

However, Riley more than compensates for what I see as his bad take on migration. Notably, he tears into the main-stream media's coverage of Trump, pointing out their obsession with the man's largely imaginary racism and the fact that his administration's economic successes were "usually credited to (actions taken by) the previous administration." Some of Riley's examples of this were glaring enough to actually surprise me.

For example, in 2019 Goldman Sachs released a major report showing that earnings for those at the bottom end of the U.S. wage distribution—where many minorities are concentrated—were rising at "nearly double the rate of pay for those at the upper end." Riley notes, rather politely, that the business-focused CNBC provided substantial coverage of the paper but that the findings were "largely ignored" by virtually all other major media outlets. This same sort of coverage of Trump's team took place across other arenas of governance, with the *Washington Post* falsely claiming that counties which hosted a Trump rally witnessed a 226 percent increase in hate crime.[3]

This performance—91 percent negative coverage of a sitting U.S. president, who was universally described as an incompetent bigot—was not an outlier within today's media environment. We have known at least since Pew (2004) that the American national media is composed roughly of 7 percent conservative and of 93 percent leftists, liberals, and (mostly left-leaning) moderates.[4]

As a result of slanted coverage of this kind, many Americans believe some truly unusual things. According to a recent survey project from the Skeptic Research Center, 32 percent of American leftists ("I am very liberal") believe that the number of unarmed black men killed by American police in a typical year is "about 1,000.[5]" An additional 14–15 percent believe that this figure is "about 10,000," and 8 percent believe it is *more than that*. In reality, the total number of unarmed black victims of fatal police shootings was 17 in the most recent year fully on record.[6] At the other end of the spectrum, among business-suited conservative types, many people are beginning to simply ignore everything the media and its anointed experts have to say. I have written about this phenomenon myself,[7] and a more in-depth 2021 survey by Reuters found that just 29 percent of Americans say they trust the mainstream media even "most of the time."[8]

This earned loss of trust may be the story of our time, and Riley covers it well via his case study of the treatment of Trump. While not perfect—I am an unabashed fan of "borders" myself—his broader essay accurately summarizes modern political trends I often observe in my professional role, from minority conservatism to voters focusing on quality of life rather than 'woke' issues. Perhaps most important, Riley makes a one-sentence point worth remembering: poor and dark-skinned voters are not idiots and, when they vote for someone, the probable reason is that they logically want to do so.

CHAPTER 6

A Response to Williams and Reilly

≳≲

JASON L. RILEY

JUAN WILLIAMS acknowledges that the workforce participation of blacks and Hispanics rose during Donald Trump's presidency, and that their unemployment and poverty rates fell to record lows. But he maintains that Trump's predecessor, Barack Obama, deserves the real credit.

According to Williams, "most of the improvement took place under President Obama," which is true to some extent but misleading. What's also true, as I wrote earlier in this volume, is that "these trends not only continued but accelerated and did so despite the expectations at the time." Williams suggests that the trendlines were destined to continue in the right direction no matter who succeeded Obama, but that was not the consensus view of government officials, academics, or the liberal commentariat when Trump entered the Oval Office.

As I noted in chapter 1, the economy Trump inherited was in fact cooling off, and the chatter was that the country could slip into another recession, especially if Trump succeeded in moving forward with conservative tax and regulatory reforms. In 2016, Obama's final year in office, economic growth fell by close to 50 percent, from 3.1 percent to 1.6 percent. The Federal Reserve projected that growth would fluctuate somewhere between 1.7 percent and 2.2 percent over the next three years, and that unemployment wouldn't get below 4.4 percent. The Congressional Budget Office said that job growth would slow, not accelerate, and that labor force participation rates would decline due in part to "lingering effects of the 2007–2009 recession and ensuing weak recovery" under Obama.

The pre-Covid economy on Trump's watch defied these forecasts. Annual growth reached 2.9 percent in 2018, which was higher than it had been during Obama's two terms. And growth never fell below 2.2 percent, which was the high end of the Fed's forecast. The economy produced *twice as many jobs* as the CBO had predicted, labor force participation rose, and unemployment shrank to 3.6 percent by the end of 2019, which was well below projections. Instead of a recession, we got a burst of economic activity, and the benefits redounded as never before to minorities.

As noted previously, between 2017 and 2019, median household incomes grew by 15.4 percent among blacks, but only by 11.5 percent among whites. Citing Bureau of Labor Statistics figures, the *Wall Street Journal* editorial page reported that during the first 11 quarters of the Trump presidency, wages for workers at the bottom rose at *more than double* the rate that they did during Obama's second term. Over the same period, less-educated workers, such as those with just a high school degree or only some college, saw their wages rise *at triple the rate* of the same group of workers during Obama's second term. Giving Obama most of the credit for *far better* economic outcomes that occurred *after* he left office is a stretch. It's also somewhat disingenuous. Williams is offering a kind of heads-I-win-tails-you-lose analysis. Liberals are eager *credit* Obama for the economy's pre-Covid performance under Trump, but who believes they would have *blamed* Obama if things had gone sideways?

≳≲

WILFRED REILLY largely agrees with my assessment of black progress under Trump and why it can be distinguished from what occurred under Obama. However, he says that I underestimate the extent to which low-skill foreign labor is "driving down pay for Americans," and that Trump's hardline stance on immigration was thus both warranted and effective.

Before we can assess whether the Trump administration's immigration restrictionism was a boon for American workers, we first need to establish that immigration—legal or illegal—in fact fell on Trump's watch. Reilly takes it as a given that it did, and then argues that working-class blacks were a major beneficiary as a result. My read of Trump's record on immigration is that his bark was bigger than his bite. No "beautiful wall" ever got built along the border with Mexico. No mass deportations ever took place. Illegal immigration, as measured by border apprehensions, *rose* sharply on Trump's watch before Covid. Deportations *declined* from the levels we saw under Obama, and the size of the unauthorized population in the United States remained largely stable. Under Trump, *legal* immigration increased as well, even as wages for less-skilled workers were rising fastest, and rates of unemployment and poverty for blacks and Hispanics were dropping to historic lows.

Put another way, the performance of the economy under Trump between 2017 and 2019 goes a long way toward refuting his claims (and Reilly's) that immigrant labor poses a significant harm to U.S. workers of any race, ethnicity, or class. The labor force grew between 2017 and 2019, yet overall unemployment dipped to a fifty-year low. In April 2019, the number of job openings exceeded the number of unemployed Americans by the largest margin on record at that time. No matter how many people Trump and Reilly believe were in the country illegally, we still had a *labor shortage* and significant *wage growth*. That's not an argument in favor of illegal immigration—correlation isn't causation—but it does strongly suggest that shielding domestic labor markets from foreign workers isn't essential to lowering unemployment rates, lifting wages, or producing faster economic growth. Nor, it seems, is the labor protectionism that Reilly applauds a critical component of black upward mobility.

Reilly says my claim that immigrant workers don't have much impact on the wages of natives is "wanting for evidence," but I purposely cited a variety of empirical studies to support that conclusion. Some of the studies are decades old, and some are more recent. Some focus on national trends, and others focus on a single region or state or locality. Some were published by immigration skeptics, others by advocates. Some found negative wage effects, and others found positive wages effects. Cumulatively, however, what the economic literature demonstrates is that immigration's wage effects, *in either direction*, are relatively small.

To support his assertion that immigration significantly harms pay for native workers, Reilly references a 2018 Pew Research Center paper titled, "For Most U.S. Workers, Real Wages Have Barely Budged in Decades."[1] He then quickly moves on as if this finding is the final word on the matter, when in fact wage stagnation continues to be one of the most hotly debated topics in economics. This isn't the place to hash out the counterarguments in detail, but I will note that a 2020 paper by the Cato Institute is titled, "The Annoying Persistence of the Income Stagnation Myth."[2] George Mason University economist Donald Boudreaux also challenges this narrative, as do W. Michael Cox and Richard Alm in their outstanding book, *Myths of Rich and Poor*.[3] The American Enterprise Institute's Michael Strain devoted an entire chapter to the topic in *The American Dream Is Not Dead*, where he wrote: "Here's the bottom line: Wages for typical workers have not stagnated for decades. Typical workers have not worked for several decades without a pay increase. A 34 percent increase in purchasing power over the last 30 years is not reasonably described as stagnant growth."[4] Finally, the economist Thomas Sowell includes a biting assessment of the supposed decades-long wage stagnation in his book, *Economic Facts and Fallacies*.[5] (Spoiler alert: Sowell finds the arguments fallacious.)

It is worth noting that even the Pew document that Reilly references acknowledges that there's another side to the story. "Wage stagnation has been a subject of much economic analysis and commentary," reads the report, "though perhaps predictably there's little agreement about what's causing it (or, indeed, whether the [Bureau of Labor Statistics] data adequately capture what's going on)." But even if Reilly could somehow persuade skeptics like me that real wages haven't risen "since 1973," he still needs to present evidence that too many foreigners in the United States working for lower wages is the main reason. Far more American women than foreign workers have entered the labor force over the past half-century, and many women opt for jobs with lower average earnings. Does Reilly think these working women are detrimental to U.S. wage growth as well?

Social and economic inequality has had many causes historically, but in the twenty-first century it is primarily driven by the underdevelopment of human capital within a group. Tempting though it may be to find excuses (racism) or scapegoats (immigrants) to explain why some groups lag and others excel, it's not at all clear that focusing on such matters, as opposed to prioritizing self-development, is the most effective way of helping people advance. That's probably something Juan, Wilfred, and I agree on in the main, and this is a better book because of their thoughtful contributions.

Notes

꘎

INTRODUCTION

1. Thomas Sowell, *The Economics and Politics of Race* (New York: Quill, 1983), 168.
2. Eric Foner, *A Short History of Reconstruction, 1863–1877* (New York: Harper Perennial, 2015), 124.
3. Ibid., 151.
4. Ibid., 154.
5. Juliet Eilperin, "What's Changed for African Americans since 1963, by the Numbers," *Washington Post*, August 22, 2013, https://www.washingtonpost.com/news/the-fix/wp/2013/08/22/whats-changed-for-african-americans-since-1963-by-the-numbers/.
6. Stephan Thernstrom and Abigail Thernstrom, *America in Black and White: One Nation, Indivisible* (New York: Simon & Schuster, 1997), 238.
7. Richard K. Vedder, "Black Economic Progress in America," *The Independent Review* 26, no. 2 (Fall 2021).
8. Robert D. Putnam and Shaylyn Romney Garrett, *The Upswing: How America Came Together a Century Ago and How We Can Do It Again* (New York: Simon & Schuster, 2020), 203.
9. Ibid., 210.
10. See, for example, Jason L. Riley, "Trump Follows Obama's Example of Moral Equivalence," *Wall Street Journal*, August 15, 2017, https://www.wsj.com/articles/trump-follows-obamas-example-of-moral-equivalence-1502836445; Jason L. Riley, "The Recovery Needs Immigrants," *Wall Street Journal*, May 12, 2020, https://www.wsj.com/articles/the-recovery-needs-immigrants-11589322270; Jason L.

Riley, "This Time, Trump's Impeachment Is Warranted," *Wall Street Journal*, January 12, 2021, https://www.wsj.com/articles/this-time-trumps-impeachment-is-warranted-11610494275; Jason L. Riley, "Trump Is More Than Just Politically Incorrect," *Wall Street Journal*, June 21, 2016, https://www.wsj.com/articles/trump-is-more-than-just-politically-incorrect-1466550500.

CHAPTER 1

1. David Brooks, "The G.O.P. Is Getting Even Worse," *New York Times*, April 23, 2021.

2. David Brooks, "The Republican Fausts," *New York Times*, January 31, 2017.

3. L. V. Anderson, "2016 Was the Year White Liberals Realized How Unjust, Racist, and Sexist America Is," *Slate*, December 29, 2016, https://slate.com/human-interest/2016/12/2016-was-the-year-white-liberals-learned-about-disillusionment.html.

4. David Remnick, "An American Tragedy," *The New Yorker*, November 9, 2016, https://www.newyorker.com/news/news-desk/an-american-tragedy-2.

5. Joe Concha, "The Washington Post: Democracy Dies in Darkness," *The Hill*, February 22, 2017.

6. Jim Rutenberg, "The Challenge Trump Poses to Objectivity," *New York Times*, August 8, 2016.

7. Jay Rosen, "Donald Trump Is Crashing the System: Journalists Need to Build a New One," *Washington Post*, July 13, 2016.

8. Martin Gurri, "Slouching Toward Post-Journalism," *City Journal*, Winter 2021.

9. Matthew Yglesias, "What Really Happened in 2016, in 7 Charts," *Vox*, September 18, 2017.

10. Nate Cohn, "Turnout Was Not Driver of Clinton's Defeat," *New York Times*, March 29, 2017.

11. Avik Roy, "No, Trump Didn't Win 'The Largest Share of Non-White Voters of Any Republican in 60 Years,'" *Forbes*, November 9, 2020; Ashitha Nagesh, "US Election 2020: Why Trump Gained Support Among Minorities," *BBC News*, November 22, 2020.

12. Elizabeth Findell, "Latinos on the Border Shifted to GOP," *Wall Street Journal*, November 9, 2020.
13. Reuben Brigety, "Donald Trump Is a Nazi Sympathizer," *Business Insider*, August 20, 2017.
14. Eric Levitz, "David Shor on Why Trump Was Good for the GOP and How Dems Can Win in 2022," *New York*, March 3, 2021.
15. Stephanie Muravchik and Jon A. Shields, *Trump's Democrats* (Washington, DC: Brookings Institution Press, 2020), 6.
16. Eric Levitz, "David Shor on Why Trump Was Good for the GOP and How Dems Can Win in 2022," *New York*, March 3, 2021.
17. Ibid.
18. Eduardo Porter, "The Bad News Is the Good News Could Be Better," *New York Times*, September 14, 2016.
19. Robert J. Barro, "The Reasons Behind the Obama Non-Recovery," *Wall Street Journal*, September 21, 2016.
20. Ibid.
21. "Great Recession, Great Recovery?" *Monthly Labor Review*, April 2018, https://www.bls.gov/opub/mlr/2018/article/great-recession-great -recovery.htm.
22. "Unemployment Rate: Black or African American," FRED Economic Data, May 2021, https://fred.stlouisfed.org/series/LNS14000006; "Unemployment Rate: White," FRED Economic Data, May 2021, https://fred.stlouisfed.org/series/LNU04000003.
23. "Historical Income Tables: Households," US Census Bureau, September 8, 2020, https://www.census.gov/data/tables/time-series/demo/income -poverty/historical-income-households.html. Incomes are in 2019 dollars.
24. "Historical Poverty Tables: People and Families—1959 to 2019," US Census Bureau, April 2021, https://www.census.gov/data/tables/time -series/demo/income-poverty/historical-poverty-people.html.
25. "Housing Vacancies and Homeownership," US Census Bureau, https:// www.census.gov/housing/hvs/data/index.html.
26. "Unemployment Rate: Black or African American," FRED Economic Data, May 2021, https://fred.stlouisfed.org/series/LNS14000006.
27. "Unemployment Rate—20 Yrs. & Over, Black or African American Men," FRED Economic Data, May 2021, https://fred.stlouisfed.org /series/LNS14000031.

28. "Labor Force Participation Rate—Black or African American," FRED Economic Data, June 13, 2021, https://fred.stlouisfed.org/series /LNS11300006.

29. Jaweed Kaleem, Kurtis Lee, and Jenny Jarvie, "America Just Spent 8 Years with a Black President: For Many African Americans, It Meant One Big Thing: Freedom to 'Dream,'" *Los Angeles Times*, January 16, 2017.

30. Ibid.

31. Emily Birnbaum, "Obama: When You Hear Economy Is Improving, 'Remember Who Started It,'" *The Hill*, October 22, 2018.

32. Tyler Pager, "Biden Says Trump Squandered Economic Expansion Begun With Obama," *Bloomberg News*, June 8, 2020, https://www.bloomberg .com/news/articles/2020-06-08/biden-says-trump-squandered -economic-expansion-begun-with-obama?sref=zlXcQw6H.

33. "Unemployment Rate," FRED Economic Data, May 2021, https:// fred.stlouisfed.org/series/UNRATE.

34. "Real Median Household Income in the United States," FRED Economic Data, September 2020, https://fred.stlouisfed.org/series /MEHOINUSA672N.

35. "Real Gross Domestic Product," FRED Economic Data, June 26, 2021. https://fred.stlouisfed.org/series/A191RL1A225NBEA.

36. Eduardo Porter, "The Bad News Is the Good News Could Be Better," *New York Times*, September 14, 2016.

37. "Chair's FOMC Press Conference Projections Materials," December 14, 2016, https://www.federalreserve.gov/monetarypolicy/files /fomcprojtabl20161214.pdf.

38. Joshua Montes, "Labor Market Projections," Congressional Budget Office, February 2, 2017, https://www.cbo.gov/publication/52393.

39. Ibid.

40. Mark Zandi, Chris Lafakis, Dan White, and Adam Ozimek, "The Macroeconomic Consequences of Mr. Trump's Economic Policies," Moody's Analytics, June 17, 2016. https://www.economy.com/mark -zandi/documents/2016-06-17-Trumps-Economic-Policies.pdf.

41. Simon Johnson, "The Consequences of a Trump Shock," Project Syndicate, October 29, 2016, https://www.project-syndicate.org

/commentary/economic-consequences-of-trump-victory-by-simon
-johnson-2016-10.

42. Matt Krantz, "Trump's Turn? Republican Presidents Rule Recessions," *USA Today*, November 20, 2016.

43. Paul Krugman, "The Economic Fallout," *New York Times*, November 9, 2016.

44. Brian Riedl interview with the author, January 25, 2021.

45. Casey B. Mulligan, *You're Hired: Untold Successes and Failures of a Populist President* (Alexandria, VA: Republic, 2020), 88.

46. Kevin A. Hassett and Aparna Mathur, "Taxes and Wages," American Enterprise Institute, June 2006, https://www.aei.org/wp-content/uploads/2011/10/20060706_TaxesandWages.pdf.

47. "The Wages of Corporate Taxes," *Wall Street Journal*, October 24, 2017.

48. N. Gregory Mankiw, "How to Improve the Trump Tax Plan," *New York Times*, November 5, 2017.

49. Casey B. Mulligan and Tomas J. Philipson, "A Turnabout on Corporate Taxes," *Wall Street Journal*, October 25, 2017.

50. Sam Batkins, "600 Major Regulations," American Action Forum, August 6, 2016.

51. Sam Batkins, "Obama Administration Issued $157 Billion in Midnight Regulation," American Action Forum, January 23, 2017, https://www.americanactionforum.org/insight/obama-administration-issued-157-billion-midnight-regulation/#ixzz6zUBlLKjL.

52. Christa Marshall, "Battle Over Obama's Rules Hits the Home Stretch," *E&E News*, April 8, 2016, https://www.eenews.net/stories/1060035325.

53. Douglas Holtz-Eakin, interview with the author, January 29, 2021.

54. Keith B. Belton and John D. Graham, "Deregulation Under Trump," *Regulation*, Summer 2020, https://www.cato.org/regulation/summer-2020/deregulation-under-trump.

55. Douglas Holtz-Eakin, interview with the author, January 29, 2021.

56. Americans for Tax Reform, "List of Tax Reform Good News," June 29, 2020, https://www.atr.org/sites/default/files/assets/Tax%20Cut%20Good%20News%20List%20Ordered%20By%20Letter.pdf.

57. Tom DiChristopher, "Exxon Mobile Announces $35 Billion in New Investments Over 5 Years, Citing Tax Reform," CNBC, January 29, 2018, https://www.cnbc.com/2018/01/29/exxon-mobil-to-invest-50-billion-in-us-over-5-years-citing-tax-reform.html.

58. "Status and Trends in the Education of Racial and Ethnic Groups," National Center for Education Statistics, February 2019, https://nces.ed.gov/programs/raceindicators/indicator_rfa.asp.

59. "Labor Force Statistics from the Current Population Survey," US Bureau of Labor Statistics, January 22, 2021, https://www.bls.gov/cps/cpsaat18.htm.

60. "Household Income in the U.S.—Percentage Distribution by Ethnic Group 2019," Statista Research Department, January 20, 2021, https://www.statista.com/statistics/203207/percentage-distribution-of-household-income-in-the-us-by-ethnic-group/.

61. "Changes in U.S. Family Finances from 2016 to 2019: Evidence from the Survey of Consumer Finances," *Federal Reserve Bulletin* 106, no. 5 (September 2020), https://www.federalreserve.gov/publications/files/scf20.pdf.

62. "The Economy's Inequality Dividend," *Wall Street Journal*, January 11, 2020.

63. Robert E. Weems, *Desegregating the Dollar: African American Consumerism in the Twentieth Century* (New York: New York University Press, 1998), 72.

64. Ben J. Wattenberg, *The Real America: A Surprising Examination of the State of the Union* (New York: Doubleday & Company, 1974), 124, 134.

65. Ibid., 137.

66. Nicholas Eberstadt, *Men Without Work: America's Invisible Crisis* (West Conshohocken, PA: Templeton Press, 2016), 72.

67. Thomas Sowell, *Discrimination and Disparities* (New York: Basic Books, 2019), 116.

68. Stephan Thernstrom and Abigail Thernstrom, *America in Black and White: One Nation, Indivisible* (New York: Simon & Schuster, 1997), 162.

69. Robert D. Putnam and Shaylyn Romney Garrett, *The Upswing: How America Came Together a Century Ago and How We Can Do It Again* (New York: Simon & Schuster, 2020), 222, 223.

70. Ibid., 203.

71. Ibid., 210.

72. Shaylyn Romney Garrett and Robert D. Putnam, "Why Did Racial Progress Stall in America?" *New York Times*, December 6, 2020.

73. Wendy Wang and W. Bradford Wilcox, "State of Contradiction: Progressive Family Culture, Traditional Family Structure in California," Institute for Family Studies, 2020, https://ifstudies.org/ifs-admin /resources/ifs-stateofcontradiction-final-1.pdf.

74. Patrik Jonsson, "Trump's Surprising Multiracial Appeal: Lessons for Both Parties," *Christian Science Monitor*, December 1, 2020.

75. Ibid.

76. Richard V. Burkhauser, Kevin Corinth, and Douglas Holtz-Eakin, "Policies to Help the Working Class in the Aftermath of COVID-19: Lessons from the Great Recession," IZA Institute of Labor Economics, March 2021, https://www.iza.org/publications/dp/14166/policies -to-help-the-working-class-in-the-aftermath-of-covid-19-lessons-from -the-great-recession.

77. Burkhauser, et al., "Policies to Help the Working Class."

78. Martha Ross and Nicole Bateman, "Disability Rates Among Working-Age Adults Are Shaped by Race, Place and Education," Brookings Institution, May 15, 2018, https://www.brookings.edu/blog/the-avenue /2018/05/15/disability-rates-among-working-age-adults-are-shaped -by-race-place-and-education/.

79. Burkhauser, et al., "Policies to Help the Working Class."

80. Burkhauser, et al., "Policies to Help the Working Class."

81. Richard V. Burkhauser, interview with the author, February 3, 2021.

82. Mike Solon, interview with the author, April 8, 2021.

83. "Economic Report of the President," February 2020, 72–73. https:// www.govinfo.gov/content/pkg/ERP-2020/pdf/ERP-2020.pdf.

84. Ibid., 67.

85. Ibid., 67–68.

86. Neil Irwin, "The Most Important Thing Biden Can Learn From the Trump Economy," *New York Times*, January 11, 2021.

87. Kevin A. Hassett, "5 Questions for Tyler Goodspeed," *National Review*, December 21, 2020, https://www.nationalreview.com/2020/12 /5-questions-for-tyler-goodspeed/.

88. Jim Powell, *FDR's Folly: How Roosevelt and His New Deal Prolonged the Great Depression* (New York: Three Rivers Press, 2003), xi.

89. Thernstrom and Thernstrom, *America in Black and White*, 187.

90. Ibid., 187–88.

91. Shelby Steele, "The Promise of President Trump," *Wall Street Journal*, January 20, 2017.

CHAPTER 2

1. James Hohmann, "What If America's Future Looks More Like Florida Than California," *Washington Post*, June 11, 2021.

2. Benjamin Franklin, *Writings*, ed. J. A. Leo Lemay (New York: Library of America, 1987), 372.

3. Richard K. Vedder and Lowell E. Gallaway, *Out of Work: Unemployment and Government in Twentieth-Century America* (New York: New York University Press, 1997), 67.

4. David E. Bernstein, *Only One Place of Redress: African Americans, Labor Regulations, and the Courts From Reconstruction to the New Deal* (Durham, NC: Duke University Press, 2001), 67.

5. Ilya Somin, "Frederick Douglass on Immigration," *Washington Post*, April 10, 2014.

6. Cited in Robert Malloy, "'Cast Down Your Bucket Where You Are,' Black Americans on Immigration," Center for Immigration Studies, June 1, 1996, https://cis.org/Report/Cast-Down-Your-Bucket-Where -You-Are-Black-Americans-Immigration.

7. Ibid.

8. David R. Henderson, "The Case for More Immigration," Hoover Institution, March 6, 2019, https://www.hoover.org/research/case -more-immigration?utm_source=Hoover%20Daily%20Report&utm _campaign=adda82foaa-Hoover%20Daily%20Report&utm_medium =email&utm_term=0_21b1edff3c-adda82foaa-72781481.

9. Richard K. Vedder, "Immigration Doesn't Displace Natives," *Wall Street Journal*, March 28, 1994.

10. Madeline Zavodny, "Immigration, Unemployment and Labor Force Participation in the United States," National Foundation for Ameri-

can Policy, May 2018, https://nfap.com/wp-content/uploads/2018/05
/IMMIGRANTS-AND-JOBS.NFAP-Policy-Brief.May-2018-1.pdf.

11. Julian L. Simon, *The Economic Consequences of Immigration*, 2nd ed. (Ann Arbor: University of Michigan Press, 1999), 241–42.

12. Ibid., 242.

13. George J. Borjas, *We Wanted Workers: Unraveling the Immigration Narrative* (New York: W. W. Norton & Company, 2016), 142.

14. Giovanni Peri, "Do Immigrant Workers Depress the Wages of Native Workers?" IZA World of Labor 2014: 42, https://wol.iza.org/articles /do-immigrant-workers-depress-the-wages-of-native-workers/long.

15. National Center for Education Statistics, "Trends in High School Dropout and Completion Rates in the United States," https://nces.ed .gov/programs/dropout/ind_01.asp.

16. "Rising Educational Attainment Among Blacks or African Americans in the Labor Force, 1992 to 2018," *The Economics Daily*; Bureau of Labor Statistics, February 13, 2019, https://www.bls.gov/opub /ted/2019/rising-educational-attainment-among-blacks-or-african -americans-in-the-labor-force-1992-to-2018.htm.

17. Nicholas Eberstadt, *Men Without Work: America's Invisible Crisis* (West Conshohocken, PA: Templeton Press, 2016), 76.

18. Amita Kelly, "Fact Check: Have Immigrants Lowered Wages for Blue-Collar American Workers?" *National Public Radio*, August 4, 2017, https://www.npr.org/2017/08/04/541321716/fact-check-have-low -skilled-immigrants-taken-american-jobs.

19. Eugene Scott, "Trump's Claim That Black Americans Are Hurt Most by Illegal Immigration Gets Pushback," *Washington Post*, January 9, 2019.

20. Paul Bedard, "Trump Keeps Jobs for Americans, Stalls Chain Migration, with New Immigration Pause," *Washington Examiner*, June 22, 2020.

21. "Civilian Labor Force in the United States from 1990 to 2020," Statista Research Department, January 22, 2021, https://www.statista.com /statistics/191750/civilian-labor-force-in-the-us-since-1990/.

22. Kimberly Amadeo, "Unemployment Rate by Year Since 1929 Compared to Inflation and GDP," The Balance, March 16, 2012, https:// www.thebalance.com/unemployment-rate-by-year-3305506.

23. "Nationwide Illegal Alien Apprehensions Fiscal Years 1925–2019," United States Border Patrol, https://www.cbp.gov/sites/default/files/assets /documents/2020-Jan/U.S.%20Border%20Patrol%20Total%20 Apprehensions%20%28FY%201925%20-%20FY%202019%29 .pdf, accessed July 29, 2021; John Gramlich, "Migrant Encounters at U.S.-Mexico Border Are at a 21-Year High," Pew Research Center, August 13, 2021, https://www.pewresearch.org/fact-tank/2021/08/13 /migrant-encounters-at-u-s-mexico-border-are-at-a-21-year-high/.

24. Randy Capps, Julia Gelatt, Ariel G. Ruiz Soto, and Jennifer Van Hook, "Unauthorized Immigrants in the United States: Stable Numbers, Changing Origins," Migration Policy Institute, December 2020, https:// www.migrationpolicy.org/research/unauthorized-immigrants-united -states-stable-numbers-changing-origins.

25. "Even as the U.S. Unauthorized Immigrant Population Remains Steady in Size, Its Composition Is Shifting, MPI Finds," Migration Policy Institute, December 17, 2020, https://www.migrationpolicy.org/news /unauthorized-immigrants-stable-numbers-changing-origins.

26. Steven A. Camarota, "There Really Has Been a Trump Effect on Immigration," *National Review*, October 28, 2020, https://www .nationalreview.com/2020/10/there-really-has-been-a-trump-effect-on -immigration/#slide-1.

27. "U.S. Immigrant Population and Share over Time, 1850–Present," Migration Policy Institute, https://www.migrationpolicy.org/programs /data-hub/charts/immigrant-population-over-time, accessed July 28, 2021.

28. Walter E. Williams, *Race and Economics: How Much Can Be Blamed on Discrimination?* (Stanford, CA: Hoover Institution Press, 2011), 31–32.

29. Jack Strauss, "Allies, Not Enemies: How Latino Immigration Boosts African American Employment and Wages," American Immigration Council, June 12, 2013, https://www.americanimmigrationcouncil .org/research/allies-not-enemies-how-latino-immigration-boosts -african-american-employment-and-wages.

30. "Table 39. Aliens Removed or Returned: Fiscal Years 1892 to 2019," Department of Homeland Security, October 28, 2020, https://www .dhs.gov/immigration-statistics/yearbook/2019/table39.

31. Stuart Anderson, interview with the author, August, 3, 2021.

32. Alex Nowrasteh, interview with the author, December 4, 2020.

33. Sarah Chaney, "Jobs Outnumber Seekers by Record Gap," *Wall Street Journal*, June 11, 2019.

CHAPTER 3

1. Jeff Cox, "Workers at the Lower End of the Pay Scale Finally Are Getting the Most Benefit From Rising Wages," CNBC, March 13, 2019, https://www.cnbc.com/2019/03/13/workers-at-lower-end-of-pay-scale-getting-most-benefit-from-rising-wages.html.

2. Paul Davidson, "Trump Touted Low-Wage Worker Pay Gains But Much of the Credit Goes to State Minimum Wage Hikes," *USA Today*, February 7, 2020.

3. Ernie Tedeschi, "Pay Is Rising Fastest for Low Earners. One Reason? Minimum Wages," *New York Times*, January 3, 2020.

4. Ryan Nunn and Jay Shambaugh, "Whose Wages Are Rising and Why?" Brookings Institution, Washington, DC, January 21, 2020, https://www.brookings.edu/policy2020/votervital/whose-wages-are-rising-and-why/.

5. Ellora Derenoncourt and Claire Montialoux, "Minimum Wages and Racial Inequality," August 31, 2020, https://gspp.berkeley.edu/assets/uploads/research/pdf/Minimum_Wages_and_Racial_Inequality.pdf.

6. "Characteristics of Minimum Wage Workers, 2017," BLS Reports, March 2018, https://www.bls.gov/opub/reports/minimum-wage/2017/home.htm.

7. Liam Sigaud and Michael Saltsman, eds., "Fighting $15? An Evaluation of the Evidence and a Case for Caution," Employment Policies Institute, Washington, DC, 2019, https://epionline.org/app/uploads/2019/01/EPI_Bookv5.pdf.

8. David Neumark and William Wascher, "Minimum Wages and Employment: A Review of Evidence from the New Minimum Wage Research," NBER Working Paper 12663, National Bureau of Economic Research, Cambridge, MA, 2006, https://www.nber.org/system/files/working_papers/w12663/w12663.pdf.

9. David Neumark and Peter Shirley, "Myth or Measurement: What Does the New Minimum Wage Research Say about Minimum Wages

and Job Loss in the United States?" NBER Working Paper 28388, National Bureau of Economic Research, Cambridge, MA, 2021, https://www.nber.org/system/files/working_papers/w28388/w28388.pdf.

10. Paul Krugman, "Liberals and Wages," *New York Times*, July 15, 2017.

11. David Neumark, interview with the author, January 17, 2021.

12. Carmen Reinicke, "Pelosi Says $15 Federal Minimum Wage Will Be in the Bill the House Sends to Senate: Here's What You Need to Know," CNBC, February 11, 2021, https://www.cnbc.com/2021/02/11/pelosi-says-15-minimum-wage-will-be-in-house-bill-sent-to-senate-.html.

13. Congressional Budget Office, "The Budgetary Effects of the Raise the Wage Act of 2021," February 2021, https://www.cbo.gov/system/files/2021-02/56975-Minimum-Wage.pdf.

14. Joseph J. Sabia, "Mininum Wages: A Poor Way to Reduce Poverty," *Tax and Budget Bulletin,* no. 70 (March 2014), https://www.cato.org/sites/cato.org/files/pubs/pdf/tbb_70.pdf.

15. Ekaterina Jardim, Mark C. Long, Robert Plotnick, Emma van Inwegen, Jacob Vigdor, and Hilary Wething, "Minimum Wage Increases, Wages, and Low-Wage Employment: Evidence From Seattle," NBER Working Paper 23532, National Bureau of Economic Research, Cambridge, MA, 2018, https://www.nber.org/system/files/working_papers/w23532/w23532.pdf.

16. William E. Even and David A. Macpherson, "Unequal Harm: Racial Disparities in the Employment Consequences of Minimum Wage Increases," Employment Policies Institute Washington, DC, 2011, https://epionline.org/app/uploads/2014/08/even_5-2011.pdf.

17. Thomas Sowell, *Basic Economics: A Common Sense Guide to the Economy*, 5th ed. (New York: Basic Books, 2015), 232.

18. Walter Williams, *Race and Economics: How Much Can Be Blamed on Discrimination?* (Stanford, CA: Hoover Institution Press, 2011), 34.

19. David R. Henderson, *The Joy of Freedom: An Economist's Odyssey* (Upper Saddle River, NJ: Prentice Hall, 2002), 113.

20. Ellora Derenoncourt and Claire Montialoux, "To Reduce Racial Inequality, Raise the Minimum Wage," *New York Times*, October 25, 2020.

21. Robert E. Weems Jr., *Desegregating the Dollar: African American Consumerism in the Twentieth Century* (New York: New York University Press, 1998), 72.

22. Ibid., 38, 39.

23. Stephan Thernstrom and Abigail Thernstrom, *America in Black and White*, 233, 234.

24. Ibid., 233.

25. Thomas Sowell, *Economic Facts and Fallacies*, 2nd ed. (New York: Basic Books, 2011), 179.

CHAPTER 4

1. Washington Post-Ipsos poll of black Americans, Jan. 2–8, 2020, https://www.washingtonpost.com/context/washington-post-ipsos-poll-of-african-americans-jan-2-8-2020/a41b5691-e181-4cda-bb88-7b31935103d9/; Yahoo News/You.gov Race and Justice poll, May 29–May 30, 1,060 U.S. Adults, https://docs.cdn.yougov.com/s23agrrx47/20200531_yahoo_race_and_justice_crosstabs.pdf; also see Andrew Romano, "Yahoo News/YouGov poll: Most Americans Say Race Was a 'Major Factor' in George Floyd's Death, but Opinions on Protests Are Split," *Yahoo News*, June 1, 2020, https://www.yahoo.com/lifestyle/yahoo-news-you-gov-poll-most-americans-say-race-was-a-major-factor-in-george-floyds-death-but-opinions-on-protests-are-split-193951336.html.

2. Joe Davidson, "Trump Says His Economic Policies Have Been Good for African Americans. Look Closer," *Washington Post*, July 13, 2020.

3. Ibid.

4. Danielle Kurtzleben, "NPR Fact Check: Trump Touts Low Unemployment Rates for African Americans, Hispanics," January 8, 2018, https://www.npr.org/2018/01/08/576552028/fact-check-trump-touts-low-unemployment-rates-for-african-americans-hispanics.

5. Hope Yen, "AP Fact Check: Trump Exaggerates His Role in Black Job Gains," July 28, 2019, https://apnews.com/article/donald-trump-business-politics-ap-fact-check-f78f4205f474482db8bb8fa7a5ebfa27.

6. Greg Robb, "Long-Standing Wealth Gap between Black and White Americans Remains Substantial, Fed Data for 2019 Show," Market-Watch, September 29, 2020, https://www.marketwatch.com/story/long -standing-wealth-gap-between-blacks-and-whites-remains-substantial -new-fed-data-for-2019-show-2020-09-28.

7. Fabiola Cineas, "No, Trump Hasn't Been the Best President for Black America since Lincoln," Vox.com, October 21, 2020, https://www .vox.com/21524499/what-trump-has-done-for-black-people.

8. See Jesse Jackson, "1984 National Democratic Convention Address," delivered July 18,1984, San Francisco, CA, https://www .americanrhetoric.com/speeches/jessejackson1984dnc.htm.

CHAPTER 5

1. Drew Desilver, "For Most U.S. Workers, Real Wages Have Barely Budged in Decades," Pew Research Center, https://www.pewresearch .org/fact-tank/2018/08/07/for-most-us-workers-real-wages-have -barely-budged-for-decades/.

2. Steven A. Camarota and Karen Zeigler, "63% of Non-Citizen Households Access Welfare Programs Compared to 35% of Native Households," Center for Immigration Studies, November 20, 2018, https://cis.org /Report/63-NonCitizen-Households-Access-Welfare-Programs.

3. Matthew Lilley and Brian Wheaton, "No, Trump Rallies Didn't Increase Hate Crimes by 226 Percent," *reason*, September 6, 2019, https:// reason.com/2019/09/06/no-trump-rallies-didnt-increase-hate-crimes -by-226-percent/.

4. Ibid.

5. "How Informed Are Americans about Race and Policing?" Research Report: CUPES-007, Civil Unrest and Presidential Election Study, February 20, 2021, https://www.skeptic.com/research-center/reports /Research-Report-CUPES-007.pdf.

6. "936 People Have Been Shot and Killed by the Police in the Past Year," *Washington Post*, September 15, 2021.

7. Wilfred Reilly, "Facts Don't Care about Your Diversity Training Certificate—A Critique of Credentialism," *Quillette*, https://quillette

.com/2021/04/04/facts-dont-care-about-your-diversity-training
-certificate-a-critique-of-credentialism/.

8. Rick Edmonds, "US Ranks Last among 46 Countries in Trust in Media,
Reuters Institute Report Finds," *Poynter*, https://www.poynter.org
/ethics-trust/2021/us-ranks-last-among-46-countries-in-trust-in
-media-reuters-institute-report-finds/.

CHAPTER 6

1. Drew Desilver, "For Most U.S. Workers, Real Wages Have Barely
Budged in Decades," Pew Research Center, August 7, 2018, https://
www.pewresearch.org/fact-tank/2018/08/07/for-most-us-workers
-real-wages-have-barely-budged-for-decades/.

2. Scott Lincicome, "The Annoying Persistence of the Income Stagnation Myth," Cato Institute, October 9, 2020, https://www.cato.org
/commentary/annoying-persistence-income-stagnation-myth.

3. W. Michael Cox and Richard Alm, *Myths of Rich and Poor* (New York:
Basic Books, 1999).

4. Michael R. Strain, *The American Dream Is Not Dead* (West Conshohocken, PA: Templeton Press, 2020), 45–46.

5. Thomas Sowell, *Economic Facts and Fallacies*, 2nd ed. (New York:
Basic Books, 2011).

About the Contributors

————————— ⋧⋦ —————————

WILFRED REILLY, PHD, is an associate professor of political science at Kentucky State University; he holds a doctorate in political science from Southern Illinois University and a law degree from the University of Illinois. Reilly is the author of *Hate Crime Hoax* (2019) and *Taboo* (2020). Reilly has published pieces in *Academic Questions*, *Commentary*, *Quillette*, and several other journals and magazines. His research interests include international relations and the prevention of war, contemporary American race relations, and modern quantitative methods to test "sacred cow" theories such as the existence of widespread white privilege.

JUAN WILLIAMS is a best-selling author and journalist. He is a political analyst for Fox News and a columnist for *The Hill*. He has published in magazines like *The Atlantic* and *Time* and writes for several newspapers, including the *Washington Post*, the *New York Times*, and the *Wall Street Journal*. Mr. Williams was born in Panama and grew up in Brooklyn, New York. He lives in Washington, DC.

About the Author

JASON L. RILEY is a senior fellow at the Manhattan Institute and a columnist for the *Wall Street Journal*, where he has published opinion pieces for more than 25 years. Riley is also a frequent public speaker and provides commentary for various television and radio news outlets.

Riley is the author of *Let Them In* (2008), *Please Stop Helping Us* (2014), *False Black Power?* (2017), and *Maverick: A Biography of Thomas Sowell* (2021). In 2021, Riley also narrated the documentary film *Thomas Sowell: Common Sense in a Senseless World*. He lives in suburban New York City.